Are You Dead Yet?

Shane Hoffman

Avid Readers Publishing Group

Lakewood, California

Avid Readers Publishing Group

http://www.avidreaderspg.com

ISBN-13: 978-1-61286-034-3

Printed in the United States

Twenty years or more since I been on my own
The days get a little darker and the nights a little
more alone
The letters get less, yet the interest still grows
Did I do it? Who's my friend? and who is my foe?
The anger is resentment and resentment smiles like
a friend
They tickled, touched, and tormented me
Is that for the Liberace showcase in the end
Are you in pain?
Are you down to your last bet?
Are you going insane?
Are you dead yet?

Dear Reader:

A little more than five years ago, I came across a package of letters written between my grandmother Nellie Koch to inmate CQ-6130 Norman Gundrum Jr. The letters were, to say, the least intriguing. I became fascinated in the simplicity of these letters as well as the earnest honesty and caring that was being written down by Mr. Gundrum.

At this point in my life, I was twenty-one years old and already had two published books. The ill-advised *All of Satan's Men* was created by a young man that had lost a relative much too soon before his life should've ended. Distraught and confused at the time, I wrote a much too personal and disillusioned book. Book idea mistake number one. Then I went off to college and never gave a

second thought to my future. It was a blast, and I wrote a purely fictional book titled *South Side of Sanity*. It was a very fun and easy book to write. To this day, I think if it was done correctly, it could've been a great book. Yet again, to publish a book with the cover the way it is and provides the synopsis I gave was at the very least, provocative and easily offensive. Book mistake number two. Then again, I was only twenty years old and never gave the nature of what I was writing about a second thought. At times, my writing style has left me vulnerable to the public and people that I shouldn't have allowed myself to be vulnerable to.

I'll never forget the moment I realized I could write a book about the infamous murder in the town that I graduated high school from. It was the summer after my sophomore year at Mansfield University. It was in the latter part of the summer. Right after the release of *South Side of Sanity*, I was more than eager and ready to write again. After writing Gundrum and receiving a letter back that he was supportive of the book, I was ecstatic. The possibilities for this book and the impact it could have never even entered my mind. To me, I finally got to write a book that is a true memoir and doesn't involve me. For the record, I reached out to people to give their opinions and facts on what happened during that time period and no one responded back. It was as though no one believed that this book was actually going to be written and published. Many people were hoping that the controversy around this topic would forever fade away. I felt disrespected.

Maybe I felt that way because I thought I was viewed as a twenty-one-year-old who couldn't make it happen. Guess what? I did.

To the folks out there that have their own version and memory of Norman Gundrum Jr. and how this horrific murder went down, I have the solution for you. Write the book yourself, how it *actually* happened. I have stated numerous times that this book is solely presented at his perspective. It is a memoir. Not a true crime novel. There's a difference. The stories and personal pain are strictly from our letters and visits.

When the book was released, I never expected the outcome that it would have. I got radio interviews from all over the country. San Diego, California, Indianapolis, Indiana, the great windy city of Chicago, The Michael Dresser Show, several newspapers and anti-bullying firms; even the college of Bloomsburg University that I was currently attending at that point. It was a great time and also a time of relief because Gundrum's story was finally out there for everyone willing to read it.

After the release of the book, Norman and I stayed in contact through letters. He even sent a birthday card to me. As time went on, the letters and the contact went from few to nothing. I'm grateful that I was able to write the book. There are many times that I still think of him and wish everything would have turned out better for him. I don't condone violent behavior, no matter how poorly the person has been mistreated by others.

Looking back on the visit and the letters, I honestly feel that this man has great remorse.

My grandmother, Nellie Koch, didn't like watching people getting picked on. I know this first hand. I was right out of kindergarten and the day was split in half between morning students and afternoon students. I was in the morning class and my distant Aunt Sandy had just dropped me off at my grandmother's house. There we watched The Young and the Restless. One of the episodes was about a guy who had left his wife and had their son with him, but decided he wanted to reconcile. He bought flowers for his reunion with his estranged wife. In a blink of an eye, he noticed his son running across the street to his mother's because he found it familiar. As the father ran onto the street, an oncoming vehicle killed him. Cheesy? Yes. Soap opera typical? Yes. Yet it mattered in the long run. Watching my grandmother's reaction left an impression to me. She was filled with genuine concern for someone other than herself. A trait she carried around her whole life.

We ate salad and mayonnaise sandwiches together. When I went out to play on the swing set, this bully would try to torment me. I remember jumping off the swing and running in with pure fear in my eye. "Where is he? Where is he?" my grandmother yelled repeatedly. She was angry and she wouldn't allow me to be bullied.

I remember that summer with her after my first grade year. She would come to my parents' house. Very patiently and sweetly, she would wake

me up. I'd stumble out and expect cereal to be made. It was. I'd lie on my father's Archie Bunker chair and eat my cereal. It was the throne. Yet, it made my grandmother uncomfortable. With the milk about to spill out, she would say in a very loving and grandmotherly voice, "SHANE! You're going to spill it!" This would happen a few times. I watched Susie Q on the Disney channel that summer. I watched my father buy the USA Today paper and follow the Cincinnati Reds that year. My mother be as perfect as a mother can be. I also watched my brother be a larger than life figure that made me feel safe.

I share this for a reason. Nellie Koch believed and maybe understood Norman Gundrum Jr. He was mistreated in a small town that had no forgiveness. He made a terrible decision. One that God can only decide. I'm not God. Hell, I'm not even a church going and God praising person. I live my life with regrets.

A few years after writing this book, I began to shy away from it. Trying to believe that it never happened. That it was a mistake. This was the book that got me attention outside of central Pennsylvania. And for a moment, it seemed that the attention and horrifying nature of it would never go away. I'm glad it didn't. I was a young and hungry author that got ahold of a story that should have been told years before I ever got the chance. For whatever reason, by fate or by mistake, I was the author that was able to tell the story. Looking back, it feels a little deeper than that. Perhaps, while writing the

story of a very troubled and hurt human being, he just needed someone to just listen to him. Someone who could, without any judgment, be there for him. I did that. For him and for me. The world can be a very scary place. In the end, it was a recipe for greatness or disaster. Depending on which sideline you stand on.

I have been asked countless amount of times whether I think Norman Gundrum Jr. killed Bobby Coup. Did he act alone? Did he plan it? And do you think he will ever be fit for society if released? I'm not the one qualified to answer these questions. I'm not a psychologist. I'm not a detective. I'm just a guy who went into a prison to interview a man doing life behind bars. A young man looking to write one of the most disgusting and provocative pieces of literature you'll ever get your hands on. As I write this, I'm sitting on my deck, enjoying a sunset, wearing cheap sunglasses with a vintage Van Halen disc playing. It is Women and Children First. Then there are the questions I can answer. Based on my personal belief.

Does Norman Gundrum need to tell the public what he feels inside? No. Does he need to satisfy anyone's thoughts? No. I won't interview him again for one reason and one reason only. I sat there face to face with him. Eye to eye. Both parties honest. There wasn't a lie or hidden secret. I was a much different person at twenty-one then I am now. One thing that hasn't changed is my honesty. Honesty and truth are very important to me. If truth is what you search, ask yourself...*Are*

You Dead Yet? As for me as a writer, you bet your ass there will be another novel. And to quote Mr. Frank Sinatra, my life can be summed up as this:

Regrets, I've had a few;
But then again, too few to mention.
I did what I had to do
And saw it through without exemption.

To Whom It May Concern:

My name is Norman Gundrum, Jr. Please be patient with me during this letter. I hope while you are reading this that you find out something about me that you never knew before, and maybe you will learn something about yourself that you never knew before as well. I am a child trapped in a man's body, a very tall child at that. I stand six feet, seven inches tall. Well, at least that's what they measured me at. Till this day, I could never understand something about myself, and I hope you can possibly help me. The question I have never been able to solve is this: am I normal, or was I born different?

You see, to you this might not seem like a logical question to ask or even a hard one at that. But for me, I never knew the answer because life was tough right from the get go. If I only had the opportunity growing up to express myself and be heard, maybe I would have never been arrested for murder. When you take time out of your day to hurt

someone, you are creating a soft spot in that person that seldom fills. We, as a society, don't see what goes through others' minds until it is unfortunately too late. That hurt has an everlasting sting to it, in a similar way when a person is allergic to bees, and they get stung by one. Now, I know I might seem a little dramatic, but the truth is *I* am a product of my surroundings.

Often times I sat and wondered what it would have been like to meet some of the girls that I never got the opportunity to talk to. Life is filled with crucial moments, including a moment that could have changed everything. Remember, I still feel like a child whose innocence was short-lived. What you encounter in this book just may frighten, disturb, and horrify you. Enter at your own risk.

The Visit

(The Righteous Shall Live by Faith)

It's strange how a thought can lead to a life-changing moment. I had been to prisons before to visit people, but somehow this time would be different, no matter how much I told myself it wouldn't. What was it that made me so intrigued by this case and its outcome? Why did I feel the need to indulge myself into this situation? Oddly enough, I didn't have the slightest answer to any of these questions, but regardless, it was something that touched me when I became involved in it.

During the late summer months, I came across a package of letters that were written between my maternal grandmother and a man by the name of Norman Gundrum, Jr. The name itself was not someone's I was familiar with. The series of events that led to his fate was something I had only heard rumors about. During the month of September, I read countless letters and researched many articles and interviews.

I knew that if I were going to write this book, I was going to have to dive deep into the raw

details and memories that surrounded this young man at the time. To take another approach would have been nothing short of the cowardly way and the inaccurate way. To me, writing a controversial book was something I had no problem doing the least bit. My entire writing career has been nothing but controversial and split between being labeled a great writer or a twisted person that doesn't realize the hurt that my thoughts have caused. I knew that this book would have to be done in a similar vein.

Deciding it was time to write him and get him to join me on this book was better than ever. I received a letter from him stating that he would finally, for the first time since the killing, tell his story. Perhaps, the story that held the most importance and one that everyone should take note of and realize the impact and truth behind this entire charade laid in his own mind. As my letters to Mr. Gundrum continued, it became more evident that I was going to visit him in prison and get to the bottom of it all.

The morning finally came that I was going to take the trip to Coal Township to visit the man doing life in prison. It was a cold Friday morning and one that I will never forget. As I woke up and dragged myself out of bed, I started to gather my belongings to head out. After getting out of the

shower, getting dressed, and deciding which cd I was going to listen to on the way, I finally headed out to Coal Township with Lynyrd Skynyrd's Street Survivors disc in my stereo.

While I was driving through the small town of Milton, Pa, I gave it a look that I perhaps never have. To me it looked like a cold town full of people that were either delusional about how much better they were than the average man and people that were just trying to get by in life doing the best they could. On my way out of the town, I passed a Lutheran church that had a sign outside that stated "The righteous shall live by faith."

Finally arriving at the prison, I was the first person there for visitation. As I walked down the hall to get to the visiting room, the walk seemed to take forever. The hallway felt like a replicate of the Wizard of Oz scene where they were finally getting to see the great Oz. It didn't take long for me to finally get in and meet Norman Gundrum, Jr. He stood at a staggering six feet, seven inches, and we proceeded to introduce ourselves. We sat down, finally braking the silence by speaking about trivial things until we got on the subject we both knew I was there for. So without further delay, here it is, the interview with Norman Gundrum, Jr. Just remember the righteous shall live by faith.

Shane Hoffman

Chapter 1
Ghost Town along the Highway

It was a small town located in central, Pennsylvania, one that was just like every single small town around the nation in that it had your usual standout points - one of those towns where every Friday night the hometown gathers at the local high school to watch the football team play - the one where nobody truly cares about the female sports unless they are on the verge of winning some rare championship.

The sad little town had lost much of its hope throughout the years. It started out as a town full of promise and job opportunities. You could possibly find the streets crowded during the weekends and holidays with shops opened up all the time. Family owned stores ran the borders of Milton and kept the people alive and happy.

Unfortunately, that was to all change drastically as the years progressed. Once what was known as the Mill Town was now filled with shut down factories and privately owned stores (now bars) and rundown churches. The opportunities

were now gone, and it was almost like a ghost town. Still though, it was a nice place to get drunk whenever one pleased and good enough to wake up on a Sunday morning and get the usual Jesus Christ fix in. What a happy little town we were! At least those were the CliffsNotes.

In every small town there are the usual social positions in the school system: the kids who are popular because their parents have money, the kids who are popular because they are really good at sports, the kids who are feared because they are the size of adult men at the age of twelve, and the kids who are bullied because of the way they look and dress. And then there is that kid that somehow sticks out like a sore thumb, and everyone just wants to fuck with for no reason. That kid was me, Norman Gundrum, Jr.

Sure, I had some qualities that were strikingly good - you know, like my height and the ability to stand up for my friends. I even tried to be as calm as one could act to hopefully sneak past all of the bullying that was going on around me. Still though, violence and heartache followed me no matter where I went. In some ways it was as though it was meant to be - never quite bothering me to the extent to where I felt the need to stand up, at least not yet.

Now I know everyone reading wants to know about the freakiness of my father and the mother that never paid attention. Well, though many of that may be true, what you don't understand is that I loved my parents. They were not perfect people. And they might not even be good people in your opinion, but I loved them.

My father was kinky and a little strange. I bet you are looking for me to tell you about those skulls he kept. Yeah, I heard those fucking stories. Or about him being a cross dresser. Yea, I heard those fucking stories. How about my mother never giving me the time of day? Yup, I have lived that too. Maybe even that she never wanted me. It is easy for you and your group to get together and run me into the ground. It doesn't take much effort. Trust me, I know how that goes. We all have those skeletons in our closet.

What I am about to tell you is something that will make your skin crawl. I lived a life on the streets that would make you blow your fucking simple little minds out. Sit back and listen to the facts I'm about to tell because it will only be told once. Just remember to ask yourself this question: Are You Dead Yet?

Shane Hoffman

Chapter 2
Welcome to the Jungle... isn't that what Milton says?

When most people die, they want to be re-membered like a hero. They want the realms of society to reflect on their good deeds and have their children tell their children that they were ideal figures. I think that idea is a little beyond insane because we just don't live those types of lives.

What will I be remembered for when the Lord runs out of fingers to count my days on? Am I just another person that fell to the wayside of society or just another figure that people used to know tell their children that they knew me? Everyone will always have their side of the story to tell, even if for the simple fact that they want the hopeless minds to surround them and give them that attention that they always craved. Even if that emotion comes by the expense of my own existence, I say, hey, that's okay.

I close my eyes, and suddenly I'm back to the year 1981. I can still hear John Lennon's *Watching the Wheels* blasting through my radio as I

lay in my room. Maybe it was that old farmhouse I used to live in, or maybe it was Jesus Christ trying to connect with me on a level before my life would turn torn beyond repair, but as I gazed out the window, a vision appeared to me unlike anything I had ever seen before or after. It was an angel.

My eyes spread wide open, my mouth too far on the ground to be brought up. I began to speak in a way that I had never before thought of. This angel represented itself to me as a messenger of God. The room had a vibe to it that I could never duplicate in feeling again. My walls seemed to have a radiant glow to them as I could feel my body become almost weightless.

For some reason or another I had no fear when I saw the extraterrestrial figure beamed down upon my body, mind, and soul. Till this day I remember telling this angel about my daily interests that included playing out back with my friend and shooting basketball. I also enjoyed a dip whenever I had the chance to get to the community pool, just to get the basics of swimming down. Little did I know that this would be the only time of my life where I'd feel that comfortable feeling of sheer safety and honesty.

My mother could hear me from down the hall speaking out like I had never done before. At

first, believing I was with one of my friends, she paid it no attention until she had finally realized that there was indeed no one in the house. She began to nervously walk down the hallway and anticipate approaching my room to find out what exactly was going on. When she finally got up to my room, she could not see anyone around and was only confronted with me sitting on the bed in a deep gaze and in conversation.

As she quietly but firmly asked, "Norman, whom are you talking to?"

I glanced up and said in a calm manner, "Don't you see, Mommy? Jesus came to visit me."

Looking onward, astonished, she asked me again, "Whom are you speaking to?"

"Jesus visited me, Mommy," I once again answered.

My mother gave me a look that no one had ever given me up until that point. The look had a sense of bewilderment and belief to it. She couldn't ignore the physical appearance or my face and how deep into concentration I was. From that day on I knew that I had someone upstairs who loved me. What wound up being the most troubling thing after my occurrence with the angel was that I couldn't ever recall its response to me. The only thing that stuck inside my mind till this day was the look the

angel had when we were together. It was a look of concern and a look of love. It was a type of look a parent gives her child when she feels the love of him at its fullest potential. That look was something I'd never forget. I'd do anything to have that back in my life, just something or someone who loved me for who I was and not for what the world knows me as.

With that moment came the feeling in life that I'm sure we all have experienced on occasion- that moment where everything suddenly becomes too dark to see and the world sees you as a whole instead of a person - a person with an outlook on life that has always been a few strokes different than the one the kid sitting next to him in class held. It was almost as though I knew from that day forward that I'd be the different one - the one that had a way of going incredibly unnoticed yet seen all at the same time. Yeah, that was me, I guess, the kid holding it inside another day so that the earth's eyes didn't focus too hard to try and figure out exactly what was going on in my mind.

The morning after just so happened to be a Sunday, and my parents and I piled into our pre-owned vehicle to get to my grandmother and grand-father Dershem's place for our weekly dinner. Those Sundays were some of the best times in my

life. They always gave me that sense of love that was always hiding at its best. The meals they would serve were some of the greatest meals a kid could possibly eat. And there was always enough to go around for seconds.

On the car rides to my grandparent's house I'd often times stare into the sky and, on occasion, close my eyes and dream about what it must be like to be a professional basketball player or maybe a swimmer giving it his all in the Olympics. It was as though being a kid meant endless possibilities. I could dream up anything that might cross my mind, and the best part was that nothing during those years seemed too far out of reach for me. Anything was possible, I thought.

Once dinner was finished and I was finally excused from the table, I'd make my way down to the lake to my Aunt's house to spend time with my cousins. That's when the games would start and the fun would officially begin. Running through the surrounded wooded area, we would play anything our minds could conjure up. Whether it was hide-and-go-seek or a game of tag, we would cherish each moment like it was our last. Being the tallest also gave me an advantage over them during tag because I had longer legs and could usually outrun them. Those days of being a kid, till this day, play

like an old cassette tape in my mind whenever I lie down and reminisce. I heard a man once say that as long as those memories are freshly lived in your mind, then those moments may never drift away too far from you to recapture.

One particular evening when my cousins and I were playing, one of my good friends that lived out near me came over and included himself in on the fun until we came across a can of blue spray paint. Picking up the can, I managed to chase my friend, Mark, around the yard and spray him with it every chance I got. After he finally ran out of breath from running, I continued to spray him really good with it. When it was all said and done, he looked just like a smurf. Mark and I didn't seem to think it was a problem until he returned home and his mother got a good look at him.

Placing Mark promptly in the trunk of the red pickup truck, his mother came racing to my house to give her two cents on how she felt about her son returning home drenched in blue spray paint. Apparently, she didn't find it nearly as funny as Mark and I because when his mom and my mom got to talking, you could almost see the steam screaming out of her ears just like in the cartoons. To hurt my case even worse, my mom had a very

mean look on her face like she was going to rip me a new one.

After Mark and his mother took off, I was subjected to a lecture on how to behave and given a stiff sentence of being grounded for two weeks in my bedroom. Though at the time the parents found it anything but humorous, with time came a certain fondness to the incident and a line of hilarious stories to follow.

During the weeks to come, I started my way into a controlled environment central Pennsylvania calls school. You know, the very first day when all the kids and their parents pile into a room and put on those fake smiles while they evaluate each kid in their mind and try to decide whether or not their kid will be better than the rest.

Each kid enters the room with that uneasy feeling. It's a feeling that tortures you inside because it's such an unsure feeling. You spent your entire life being cradled by your family, and now all of a sudden you realize that you are just another person in this world. Gazing out through the rest of the children, you find your way to the person that most resembles you. This starts to make you feel a little at ease because you found someone that is close to what you have always believed to have worked.

Unfortunately for me, I was one of those kids from the beginning that didn't have anything. People could spot me a mile away. I was tall and lengthy, and my style was less from perfect. To the world I stuck out like a sore thumb, but to me I was as small as a stone. When people make you feel like you are nothing, you begin to believe them. It starts this cycle in your mind that says you will never measure up to what everyone else has.

As the days come and go, I started to create that wall to hide me away from all of the bullying. It was a wall that was hard as rock on the outside but as thick as water on the inside. The worst part about it all was that I never quite understood why I was always the outcast. What was it about me that made the town of Milton so cruel? Kids find out early on who's got the money and who's got the short end of the stick. When that happens, each and every single individual knows what your net worth is to them. Even the children who know they aren't in that same category as the elite will start to make their rounds on torturing you because it takes away from the tension in their own lives.

Do you know what it's like to lie in your bed at night and cry - not only to cry but to wonder on a day-to-day basis what is wrong with you? The tears felt warm as they slowly but heavily swam

down my young face. Please God, take me away from this hell that I have been thrown into. Yeah, that was a daily ritual in my life; take me away from this fucking hell hole.

One of the most troubling things I have found out as I have gotten older is that people never change. The way people are when they are kids is often times how they treat the world when they get older, just in a much more subtle kind of way, I suppose. Adults still look down on the same people they have their entire lives, quite often believing in their perfect Christian minds that they are just a tad better than you will ever hope to be.

After lying in bed and soaking my pillow case with tears, I decided to come out into the kitchen and get a drink of water to hopefully calm down. Taking a seat on our countertop, I noticed my father drinking a beer in the living room watching television with the lights out.

My sobbing must have been a little loud because he asked without looking at me, "What's wrong, Norm?"

Stunned at first, I said, "Nothing."

"There's a whole lot of crying going on over nothing then," he spoke once again.

So I finally responded by telling him there were a few kids at school that were picking on me, and I didn't know how to make them stop.

"That'll all pass in good time," my father remarked. I guess at that time it was comforting to hear that statement, but unfortunately, it never proved to be true, at least not for me that is.

While talking to my father, we didn't make eye contact the entire time until I went and sat down next to him. Like I mentioned before, he was drinking, and that had me interested, to say the least. I have seen people drink before and noticed the rapid change it had in folks. It made some people happy, and it made some people angry. My father seldom drank, but when he did, it had a way of relaxing him. Curiosity had officially taken a hold of me because I wanted a taste of that beer. The desire was strong, but the outcome had me nervous inside. I thought to myself, if alcohol can improve others' lives, why can't it have the same impact on me?

Working up all the courage I could, I finally asked my father if I could have a taste of his beer.

There was a strange pause before he began to speak. "Norman, if you want a taste of my beer, I will let you. But first you must make me a promise."

"Sure Dad, anything," I answered.

"If you take a drink of this beer and you don't like it, then you must never take a drink of another beer the rest of your life. If you do like the way it tastes, then when you get a little older, you can drink till you vomit.

Eagerly, I answered quickly with a yes.

Taking that can of Old Milwaukee in my hand, it took me a few seconds to actually work up the courage and put it to my lips. I had high hopes in what alcohol could do for me. Finally, I took a big gulp of the beer like I was drinking a soda. Upon the initial meeting in my mouth, I threw it all up. That taste was nastier than anything I had ever tasted. If I had to put a direct resemblance to the taste, I would say it reminded me of horse piss. The beer was warm and reeked of bad breath. My father had a smirk on his face, knowing from the beginning that I would not prefer that awful taste. It made me wonder for the longest time why anyone would drink that poison. But I guess for some, it's an easy escape from their own reality.

Walking back into my bedroom, already dreading the next morning when I would have to return to that awful school, my father called out my name.

When I turned around, he said, "Norman, don't let anyone push you around. You only have yourself to protect."

The next day I returned to school with a mindset that I hoped would last me forever, but it only survived a few days. Upon arriving back to that dreadful classroom, I ran into a guy named Jason. Jason was this guy of average height and popularity. He had this thought in his mind that said if he liked what he liked and wanted it, then you would have a major problem with him. For whatever reason, I didn't buy any of that shit that day and decided to stand toe-to-toe with the wannabe tough asshole.

Standing in the lunch line waiting to make some excuse to the lunch lady why I couldn't afford an entire lunch, I began to talk to a pretty girl by the name of Sheena. She was this pure kind of girl. You know what I mean, right? She was pure innocence in that age old fashioned kind of way - the girl that wouldn't hurt you for the sake of seeing your reaction. She was plainly and simply the girl next door who felt a connection with a guy whose first intention wasn't taking advantage of her.

As the time passed, Jason began to think I was moving in on his precious territory and thought it necessary to approach both of us in a rudely but timely fashion. I'll never forget his remark.

"You trying to move up just a little bit, dirt bag Gundrum? I felt almost two feet tall because I didn't have a response. Only a few seconds later did he begin to tear into Sheena for conversing with me. I felt this rare burst of anger boiling through my skin. It was as though god had unleashed the hounds of hell inside my soul and wanted me to inflict those moments onto another human being.

If those thoughts from God are true, then they came to the fruits of my labor. It was as though those almost two years of constant torture and humiliation finally came through because I tackled Jason to the ground and managed to clean his punk ass clock. In Jim Croce's words, he looked like a jigsaw puzzle with a couple of pieces gone. The inner talk that exists in my mind was telling me to get off of him and not hurt him beyond repair, and the other side of me suggested to hurt him in a way that he wouldn't waste anymore time. Fortunately, the fight ended in a modest fashion, with me winning of course.

Not only did I conquer one of my longtime goals, but I got a sense of caring and understanding by Sheena that I had never witnessed. It was well worth it in my opinion because that day was the first time I had ever been kissed. The kiss was a light but heartfelt landing on my right cheek. That day

I felt like a real man for the very first time in my life. Our friendship never ended up blossoming to the point where I wanted it to, but that really didn't matter. I got what Jason had desired from her the entire school year, and for me to get ahead in the game was a new and good feeling. Tom Petty was right: even the losers get lucky sometimes.

Unfortunately, that feeling of accomplishment didn't last too long for me. After spending only a short stint living in that old farmhouse out in West Milton, my family packed up and moved into a trailer court that went by the ever so prestigious name of Bucknell View. It wasn't the change I had been looking for, and it even made people look even further down upon me.

I was known as trailer trash, white trash, and shit. During this time, I began to develop a very embarrassing problem. For whatever reason, I couldn't control my body when it came to shitting. I would shit myself all the time. This mostly occurred because of the constant teasing that I was subjected to on a day-to-day basis. The anxiety was far more than I could handle. Every day that I had to walk into that school I had that heart-pounding, scary feeling that didn't ease the least bit. My concentration in school severely decreased as I was constantly worried about soiling myself. I can still

remember saying to myself every time I stepped foot in that classroom, *Please God, don't let this happen to me again; please don't let this happen to me again.*

In the back of my mind I wished consistently that I would just go unnoticed. Maybe the kids today will not mind me any attention and just get on with whatever they had to do. Sadly though, picking on me was what they had to do. The thought always ran through my mind that I was destined for this. Was I meant to be the one who isn't like the rest? Is this truly my own God given destiny?

Whenever you shit yourself, it doesn't take long for someone to take notice. The scent picks up in the air very quickly. Most of the time the teachers would just send me outside so they wouldn't have to handle the situation. With this new profound problem and now living in a trailer park that every-one looked down upon, my chances of ever getting Sheena were forever dashed, as well as my chances of getting anyone else my desperate mind might have considered.

As soon as the school day was over with, I'd make my dash right home where I hoped would be my getaway. That wasn't always the case. That day when upon arriving home, a kid that lived in the trailer park was making every chance to get

under my skin. This kid just kept rambling on and on about my mother, saying and doing anything he could think of just to make me angrier and angrier. I could almost handle being picked on when the subject matter consisted of me, but when he started driving my mother into the ground, the gloves finally come off.

Getting on his bike and riding off, I began to chase after him with every bit of energy I had. *Finally*, I thought, when I actually caught up to him, I managed to grab a hold of his arm and throw him off the bike. We both hit the ground hard. I pulled him under me and once again gave him the ass-kicking of his life. The fight felt good to me once it was over. Getting that raw energy out towards someone that had every intention on ruining my day and upsetting me was self-gratifying.

A few days later something happened that shocked me. This kid actually showed up to my house and apologized. I couldn't believe it; someone took the time out to say sorry for acting insensitive. Happy as can be, I gladly accepted his apology. Justin and I later became good friends. This gave me that sort of hope that one needs to get through some of the hard times. It also allowed my mind to dance with the idea that if this person stopped picking on me and became my friend, maybe others

could and would do the same thing. This instantly changed my view for awhile and gave me the courage to step back into the classrooms with the thought that something positive could come from all of this after all.

For the first time in a while, things were going roughly smooth in my life. To me, having things as smooth still meant being treated like a second class citizen and getting shit kicked up in my face. But even those times where events seem to be favoring me can quickly turn into something I could barely handle.

My parents and I often times would visit my aunt and just spend time out at her house and play games while often just sitting and bullshitting about the day. Many times I would go see my aunt, and she would see how I was doing and vice versa. Lately, we started to notice there was a change in her actions and words.

She had begun to fall into a rough patch that made her begin to drink more heavily and created a side of her that even she didn't want to pay any attention to. With her man out of her life and things progressively getting worse, she gathered those feelings we often times feel when we are alone - that we just don't seem to fit in anywhere. We start to feel like that piece of the puzzle that just doesn't

seem to belong anywhere in the grand scheme of things - the constant roaming around on this earth and trying to find something or someone that relates to you and doesn't make you feel like you are completely worthless.

It's such a hard emotion that only takes you into despair. Loneliness is the root of all disaster, in my opinion. It's that moment when you finally give in and can't seem to look far enough down the road to pull yourself out of that ditch.

It was a cloudy afternoon when it all decided to come to an abrupt change. My mother called me into the living room to break the news to me. In an instant, everything changed, like the sky got closer to the earth, and the ground began to move uncontrollably. In a soft spoken tone, she whispered, "Your aunt is dead."

I couldn't believe it; the blood in my face felt like it completely flushed out. My heart felt as though it had fallen out of my chest. My body was numb in a way I had never imagined.

My breaths became quick and hard, and the temperature in the room felt like it had dropped thirty degrees. The only thing that was warm on my body was the river of tears that followed. Each tear flooding my face with pain and agony. How could this have happened? The last memories of

her began to rush rapidly through the corridors of my mind, and it was almost like a tape being played over and over again. Maybe if one of us were there, none of this would have occurred. Just maybe this horrific tragedy wouldn't have happened.

Suicide. Suicide. Suicide. The words were ringing in the back of my mind, and I just couldn't seem to get them far enough away to get a clear thought through my mind. Is this what happens when life gets too tough to handle? Are we ultimately on a road to death that lends suicide a quick and easy fix to the solution? I just wanted to see her face again. I just wanted to see that smile light up the room just once more. If I could have only just put my hand on her cheek and say that I loved her, maybe it could have helped in the end.

It just felt like another brick in the wall. What do you really say when something like this happens to someone you know. Sorry? What a shame? She was treated like a number instead of a person, never given the time or day in anyone's life. People always wonder how something like this happens. You don't have to look any further than how you treat someone. A simple *hello* or *how are you* can make the biggest difference with people who have so little in their lives. They just want to be accepted.

I didn't know how to conceal the pain in a healthy manner so I just pretended like everything was good. It was somewhat the only way I could get through the pain on a daily basis. The teachers and counselors didn't lend a hand in trying to help me get through the pain. I think they just felt like they didn't know me enough to approach me, but you aren't going to get to know something from someone unless you take the time to get to know the whole part instead of certain pieces. Could I hold that guilt against them? Believe it or not, I didn't. I was already used to the ways of this world by my early age. So in a drastic way, it didn't hinder me anymore; it just made me more aware of the true ways of people in my surroundings.

The real monkey on her back was the out-lasting trends of this small community without a close-knit of people there to help out. Why do people always assume that others have it together? Society just has this view that they are the only ones that feel down and out at times and can't seem to get two feet on the ground when it matters the most. Never mind the people that get thrown into this world with a chip already on their shoulders. We don't think twice about them because society already assumes their destiny as being minimum

wage and staying in that trailer park that they grew up in, nothing more and nothing sure as hell less.

The anger raged inside of me like a wildfire that couldn't be stopped. I never felt such a mixture of feelings that consisted of loneliness, rage, and being lost. And the worst part of this was there was nothing I could do about it. There wasn't one mother fucking thing I could do about this. I thought about all the parties and good times we will never have a chance to have. I wouldn't get the chance to have that in my life. Not now. Not ever. Right now though, that doesn't matter.

How do we as humans deal with situations that we never quite prepare ourselves for? Making our minds believe something so wholeheartedly that we can't imagine anything other than that being true often proves harmful. Suicide is something that leaves us asking questions until the day we are dead. The thought of someone I love taking her life makes me take on a different approach to my own life. It's something I never imagine happening until it's too late. The signs which everyone finds so obvious are usually anything but. We spend so much time and energy learning how not to *feel* that when the time comes for us to deal with our emotions, we have no clue *how to* anymore. Our sleepless self-

help society has drained us of every single coping mechanism out there and has replaced them with books and pills that are written by people who don't have a clue about how to make their own lives right, let alone counsel others on their emotions and thoughts on life.

We wake up every day and put on every kind of mask we can find to hide ourselves away from the world, not realizing at the time that we are just cruising through life and not fully understanding exactly who we are. People spend their whole lives trying to figure out who they are, and they try on different faces in the process. This though is healthy. You've got to experiment and do test runs with a few different perspectives to find out which ones fit you the best. The trouble with that, however, lies within taking the perspective on yourself that everyone takes on you and decides it fits you best instead of finding the one that makes you truly you.

And in my mind, I could only help to think that alone is how the rest of my life would be. I sat at the old rock by my house like a had a million times before and threw pebbles into that old lake and just blanked out. I didn't think about anything, and I didn't feel anything. I was just numb, and that feeling was the first thing I could call mine and only

mine, my whole life it seemed. It was like nothing existed and nothing mattered. It was just this surreal dream, and I was the only thing that existed. How is that for different? After a while I thought about my aunt and the type of woman she was. I thought about the things in life she liked and the things she hated. I thought about how her days were and what could have been going through her mind when she knew she was about to die.

I woke up and got out of bed. Everything was still the same. There was no change in the wind of depression. There was no May flowers or summer sunshine beaming off of my face - just the debris of what is formerly known. Am I the only person who wanders in the walk of life not knowing where and who I am? The more I search sometimes, the less I find. Perhaps, it is the moments in life when nothing is expected or hoped for when freedom arises. I think that the most complex things in life can be broken down into small explanations. Why do we complicate what is so simple? The essence of life is not the longevity but the moments that we feel alive. We must awaken ourselves from this everyday misery and regret.

Have you ever been alone? You know what I mean, right? Have you ever sat in a bed and looked at the ceiling and just drifted off into pure thought?

I think what keeps people going in life are not the rewards of living but the fear of death - the fear of being alone - the fear of waking up and finding themselves in a mental solitary confinement.

Many times we never imagine what we find to be unthinkable. I mean, where would we be afterwards? Where would our minds take us if we let them run free and do as they pleased? Would we commit the unthinkable crimes of our youth? Or would we be disappointed to find out that some of our loved ones are emptier inside than a corpse rotting on the side of a highway? I'd like to think there are compassion, love, and understanding in every living thing on this earth. But that misleading hope has led to many a man's untimely death and mourning.

Maybe if people every now and then could look into another's soul, things would be much clearer. If someone would look into your soul what would they see or find? Everyone can look into another person's soul. The eyes are the gateway to the soul. They are the very essence to decision making. You can even look through a blind man's soul by looking into his eyes. His eyes can see, just not in the way a seeing man has been taught, not in the way we perceive the world and its functions.

I guess to everyone my life has completely changed. It's sad that it took a funeral to unconceal that. I'm so tired of everyone trying to figure me out like I'm some kind of puzzle or something. I'm just hurting inside, and there's nothing I can do to make this hurt go away. Is there anything that will make this surreal pain go away? Why do people have to scrutinize everything I say or do? Just leave me alone. Just leave me alone.

I think we all believe in something that we think will save us in the end - something in our minds that we think sets us apart from anything and everything. It is funny and strange to me that we treat people like they are nothing, and we commit more sins than a demon in hell on a regular basis. We still, however, continue to think that we are above and beyond everyone else, that our needs in some way, shape, or form are above others and that God would rather help us and knows us to be good but knows others little, as to say they are hell ridden. That is the nice way. Huh?

We follow organizations and religious groups because it gives us an identity and sense of self. We feel as though we have finally discovered where we belong and what we should be following in this world where materialism is the only thing left, and less and less people are living and dying

without love. Love is truly the only thing that has survived the test of time. All fashion trends and self-satisfying worldly possessions have all come and gone with the wind.

What's lying around you and what's eating at me are two opposite things in the nature of our world. We are just striving and living for the cause. But do we know just what that cause is, or is it just pure fun and fantasy? Do you have a deeper sense of what is real and fabrication of the mind? Well, do you? You never know when the end is near or when a beginning is about to show up right on your front door step, little miss sunshine. A shot in the heart can hit you like a ton of fucking bricks. We all should do as you say. Right? Right? Right? Right?

If it has to be, then we are all just lost souls roaming around in total darkness, looking for the road to recovery. If every love that was lost was a death in our hearts, then I guess we are just zombies looking for a reason, rhyme, or cause. What is the human heart? Why does it keep us alive? And why do we spend so much time protecting it all the while we abuse it? Is it our nature as human beings to kill and torture ourselves? We strive for goodness in ourselves, yet we look for the worst in others. Maybe we are not the good holy ones God is looking to save and heal. Maybe we are the

roadblock that keeps peace from entering into the world and solving its most hated crimes. We just never know how we feel or what we will do in times of desperation and need. It is confusing, yet it is beautiful.

It's beautiful for the watcher and confusing for the participant. It seems as though we are actors and actresses in a play that doesn't have a necessary script. We are players in the game of life and the penetrated determines the end. Yeah, that seems logical and fair. I think the best way out is not to take a deeper look into our eyes because that is where the soul is. The soul is our eyes. Our eyes tell everything about us. They let out how we feel and how far we are willing to go to get freedom and love. The soul is just right behind the eyes. The eyes are the front door way to the soul. This, friend, is a fact, not a myth or idea, but a cold hard fact. How does it all make you feel? How does it all fit in your head? Love is passion, and passion is love. Death is birth, and yet birth guarantees death. So which is sadder, birth or death? Don't let either one determine your mind or your destiny because destiny is a road to forgetfulness, which leads to the end of time. Destiny is our way of explaining the unknown and fucking the lover of evil. Am I right? Am I wrong?"

Shane Hoffman

God grant me the serenity
to accept the things I cannot change;
courage to change the things I can;
and wisdom to know the difference.

Living one day at a time;
Enjoying one moment at a time;
Accepting hardships as the pathway to peace;
Taking, as He did, this sinful world
as it is, not as I would have it;
Trusting that He will make all things right
if I surrender to His Will;
That I may be reasonably happy in this life
and supremely happy with Him
Forever in the next.
Amen.

Chapter 3
Youth Gone Wild

When you are child, you have a certain appreciation for things that later on in life seem almost pointless. Those simple ideas and jokes that made you who you were and helped pass the time along in your little one-horse town have a way of fading out throughout the years.

One of those memories for me was when I was just a little kid in elementary school and my mother would take me out for breakfast. This was a ritual she and I kept for quite some time. Every Friday before school, we would pile into our vehicle and head out to either Goodwill's in Montandon or Betsy Ross in Milton. Those sausage and eggs never tasted so good. It was those moments that allowed my heart to still beat at times. The thought of going to school and being picked on for yet another day didn't matter during those Friday morning breakfasts, plus it was the last day of the school week, which meant the weekend was on our heels, and I could escape yet again into my own fantasy world.

Upon being dropped off for school, my friend, Tim, and I met up outside class and started talking about possibly ditching school for the day. Thinking to myself how wonderful it would be to get to skip out and get an early jump on the weekend, I decided to continue to push him on the idea. Standing there, Tim had that look in his eyes that he wanted to do it, but the initial fear of his parents finding out was starting to weigh on him. Finally, after doing some influential talking, we decided that we were indeed going to skip out on Milton for the day.

Tim was one of my best friends who had a way of sticking by me during these awful times. He wouldn't judge me, and we always had clean innocent fun. A few years down the road, Tim would unfortunately pass away, so this story is for you, good friend.

With both of us knowing that our parents may possibly still be at the house, we took our good old time arriving at each one of our houses. When we got inside, we realized how boring it was just sitting around so we started to question whether or not we should have cut class. Wanting to take a risk on something, I said, "Hey Tim, let's get our bikes and ride 'em all the way to the Susquehanna mall."

At first, Tim glanced over at me like I was out of my mind, but just like skipping school, it took some convincing to pull this off. Tim wanted to do the same things I did; it was just a matter of someone coming out and saying it. Plus there was the factor of who would actually follow through with what he so proudly boasted.

During this time, none of us obviously had our driver's license so the trip to the mall would definitely have to be done on bicycles. Once again, after egging him, on both Tim and I jumped on those bikes and headed off into our great adventure to the mall. Carried with us was every cent we had. In my pocket, I held ten dollars and fifty three cents, and Tim carried a whopping seven dollars and eighteen cents. Peddling our way as fast as we could, we didn't realize or understand the meaning of pacing ourselves.

Being tired as can be, we both just kept peddling and peddling our asses off. I never realized a few miles could be so hard, even on a bicycle. The cars went whistling past us, faster and faster it seemed. For some reason, every time a tractor trailer would come whizzing our way, it took us about ten feet backwards.

After all of that time and effort, Tim and I finally made it to the mall. It was like a great long

conquest when we reached our destination. It was as though we reached the great Oz. Parking our bikes along the bike rack, we decided it was time to finally head in and have ourselves one hell of a time. We did everything we could with the little money we possessed. After roaming around the mall in almost every store we could think of, Tim and I sat down and got ourselves a few slices of pizza and some cold Mountain Dews to wash it down. We really felt like real men that day, taking responsibility into our own hands and doing what we wanted to felt nice. It was one of my first tastes of real independence for the day.

Our only mistake lay in that we should have paid a lot closer attention to the time because when Tim looked down at his watch, I could almost see his eyes bulge out of his head.

Looking at me with the most serious look he had, he said, "Norm, we need to leave right now."

"Why?" I asked?

"Because we are in Selinsgrove, and school lets out in ten minutes."

All of sudden I had that real sick feeling in the pit of my gut. "Ten minutes! Ten minutes!" I yelled once again. "Let's get the hell out of here!"

Racing through the mall as fast as we could, we almost got stopped by a mall security guard, but

luckily we just kept going right past him. We were in such a panic that we ran out of the wrong exit and thought someone had stolen our bikes. Now the panic turned into anger towards one another, both of us blaming each other for ditching school to have a little fun.

Thankfully, before the blaming game got too out of hand, we both realized that we were in the wrong parking lot and ran around to the other side to jump on those bikes like they were Harley Davidsons and got the hell out of there. I don't think Tim or I had ever peddled that fast in our entire lives. The time it took to get back home almost seemed to split right into two.

When we arrived home, no one had even noticed that we were gone the entire day, and the school had never even called home for us. They probably had hoped I dropped out by then. Though I wish I could have dropped out, Milton did come through for me on that day because that decision to not make a phone call gave me my weekend instead of sitting inside all day waiting for the grass to grow.

Looking back, that was one of the greatest times I had ever had in my entire life. Just something simple like my friend and I hitting the open road

with our big bad bicycles made all the difference in the world to me at that moment.

That weekend I decided to just lie in my bed and listen to some of my favorite music. It was a relief putting in Metallica's Kill 'Em All album and just letting the tunes drift me away in and out of reality. Something about the song No Remorse had a tight fisted grip on me. Many bands' music just didn't have that same connection. The lyrics stated:

War without end
No remorse no repent
We don't care what I meant
Another day another death
Another sorrow another breath
No remorse no repent
We don't care what it meant
Another day another death
Another sorrow another breath

Those lyrics started to become the soundtrack of my life. Music has a way of taking me out of the worst possible moments. When those rhythms start soaring through my soul, it becomes one-on-one with me. It makes me feel that there is

someone else out there that knows how I feel and understands where I am going in life.

It was starting to become that time of the season again when the town began to put up those stupid candlelights all over town and people were hustling and bustling all around trying to please their so-called loved ones by buying them presents to show it. I always felt like Charlie Brown during Christmas time. The fact that it wasn't usually a happy one for me because I could see the disappointment in my parents' eyes because they couldn't buy the things that I so desperately desired. I just wanted a Christmas where we three in the house could wake up and be happy and not focus on the terrible times and struggles we had and instead focus on the fact that we were healthy and living.

The one thing I did cherish about Christmas time was that it was a break away from school. My problems of shitting myself were only getting worse, and it was becoming harder and harder for me to control myself. The laughs echoed throughout the hallways and classrooms whenever I was spotted.

Shit pants was the name they finally decided on when calling me out. Shit pants was their favorite term to spit in my face. It was, in so many ways, humiliating for me. All of those girls that I would spend all my time trying to gather up the courage

and speak to were now something I would never even dream of anymore. No girl wants to take a chance on a guy that shits himself all of the time and doesn't even have a say in the matter.

The truth was if someone would have taken a chance on me, she would've seen how much care and love I had to offer. Many times, I wouldn't feel that at home, and it carried through for much of my life. One of the worse parts about this entire ideal situation is that the teachers would often times be spotted with smirks on their faces. Some of them tried to hide it while the other ones would chime in with the students. Those teachers that jumped in on the fun were people who, while growing up, never had any real friends and only became teachers so they could just try once again to fit in, even if that meant hurting the kids that were similar to them while growing up. I guess they didn't recognize it when they did it. It is their way of overcoming their own personal insecurities while creating ones for kids that are growing up through the system.

My parents never took me to get looked at for my shitting problem. It was a problem that began to get increasingly worse through the years. One particular event would be one to stick with me the rest of my life. Sitting in my arithmetic class, we all had to break up into groups and solve the next

ten problems in our little paperback workbook. Of course, no one picked me to be in their group, and I was always too shy to ask to be a part of one so the teacher had to put me into a group. She knew every time we all had to get into groups that she would end up putting me into one. It almost got to the point where she stopped with that idea and kept everyone doing the problems individually.

While she was walking over with that slightly heavy face that was caked in makeup and bad hair coloring, she started to get a scent of what was happening in my pants. Her eyes began to roll like they had so many times before while stating, "Norm, did you have another accident?"

"Yes, ma'am."

"Head down to the nursing station, and I'll let them know that you are on your way."

Making my way down to the nursing station, the smell followed me, and so did the remarks and put downs. It was beyond humiliating. To make matters worse, one of the girls that I had a crush on for some time spotted me and the stains that surrounded my entire pants. She just had this look of disgust on her face, kind of like she just spotted a dead body rotting. That look was the worst for me because it killed another dream of mine, that if I could get a nice popular girl to like me just a little

47

bit then maybe I wouldn't be picked on so much and maybe move on to another person or thing.

After the walk of shame, I finally made my way to the nursing station where I was met with a look of horror. Softly speaking, I said to the nurse that I needed a change of clothing because I had just soiled myself.

"Not again, Norman," she replied. "Just take a seat, and I'll be with you in just a few minutes."

Sitting there in that office, the rest of the kids waiting to see the nurse gradually got up and left because they couldn't handle the smell that was reeking through my pants. I felt so ashamed of myself. Why wouldn't this fucking stop? Why couldn't this issue just please take care of itself for once? Why me? I always thought. Why the fuck me again? I guess Charlie Brown and I had a lot more in common. I wonder if he ever met God and then shit himself.

The times arrived that the nurse would come back and think of an excuse as to why she couldn't help me. "Norman," she once again said, "we called your mother, and she will be picking you up some time very soon."

My first reaction was the thought of *why couldn't they just give me a change of clothes that they would give to any other kid that would come*

down with a problem of the same sort? Feeling timid, I just thanked her for calling my mother and sat down to wait for her, except the nurse had this look on her face like she wasn't through speaking with me. The nurse continued on by telling me that I had to wait outside until my mother arrived. Sit outside? Sit outside? I thought this was beyond fucking ridiculous.

It was the middle of December, and I had to sit outside in my shit-filled pants until my mother got there. Having that rage build up inside of me like it had so many times before, I asked her why. She told me my mother would be there very soon and there were many kids that needed to see her soon. So there I was sitting outside Milton, feeling like a complete zero. The wind started to blow on that miserable fucking winter day. *Fuck Milton,* I thought. They didn't want to help anyone who really needed it; they just liked the stupid mother fuckers who ran the school board and sat in their nice houses and drank themselves into oblivion because they had nothing else better to do.

I felt so hurt and worthless. My breathing started to become quite heavy, and the tears began to run down my cheeks and off onto my chest. I thought, *Why is this happening to me, God? Why?* It was as though my entire world was collapsing

right around me. Even the ground felt like it was starting to shake. My heart was beating in a way I could barely describe. It was one of those beats where it feels like it is ready to jump out of your chest.

On top of everything, it was brutally cold outside. I didn't possess an honest winter jacket so I closed up my shirt as much as I could. It was just one of those miserable winter days. The nurse must have been lying to me because my mom didn't show up until an hour and a half later. When she arrived, she didn't bother to ask why I was sitting outside in the cold with my pants filled with shit. She just told me to hop into the car so we could go home.

On the way home, we didn't talk about much at all. I just wanted her to walk into that school and give them pure hell. I wanted someone to stick up for me and just show someone that they just can't push me around like that. They just couldn't treat me like a piece of worthless shit. I was a person with feelings, someone who just wanted to be treated like he mattered. Was that such a terrible thing to want out of life? Was I being too unreasonable?

When I got up, I just jumped into the shower and washed away the remnants of the day. The warm water rushing onto my skin felt very soothing. Standing there, I let the day drain away from me

and let my mind run free. I couldn't help but think about that girl seeing me in that condition. *Will she remember?* I asked myself. Of course she would. Who the hell wouldn't remember such a disgusting scene? The thought of returning to school haunted me tremendously. At least it was finally Christmas vacation, and I would have ten days until I'd have to step foot back into that hell house. I must have been in the shower a little too long because I could hear my father banging on the wall for me to come out.

Heading back into my room, I lay there and stared at the ceiling. I said to myself the oh so famous quote, if it wasn't for bad luck, I'd have no luck at all. Sometimes I feel like I am living in a world that never had any plans of having me live in it. It is as though God fell asleep, and when he woke up, I was here, and he didn't have the heart to take me off the earth so he just keeps poking at me until I finally break. To you those thoughts may seem crazy, but to me they seemed more real than anything. I still searched for a glimpse of hope in it all. At least Christmas was coming up in two days, and maybe I'd get that Sega system that I wanted. If I could just sit back and play some NBA game, I'd be quite happy.

Hey God, I'm tired of finishing second to last;
There's something out there better than what's been
in my past.
I lived those years, man, they run by so damn fast;
Is the love I'm praying for going to be enough to
last?

Christmas day finally came, and as I woke up,
I had this unaware excitement running throughout
my body. The thought of possibly getting something
that I had a strong desire to get was beginning to
get a bit overwhelming. When I reached our small
living room, the Christmas tree was lit up, but the
supplies under the tree were quite limited. Getting
close to the tree, I bent down and grabbed my two
lonesome gifts. One was a pack of baseball cards,
and the other was a pack of lollyipops.

The disappointment I felt inside of me that
day was a bottomless pit type of feeling. For some
reason, I spent that entire holiday season waiting
to get that Sega system and maybe some cash to
go out and have fun with. Instead, that Christmas
was a sure sign of the rough times. As I glanced
up into my parents' eyes, I could see the obvious
embarrassment that lay in them. They were having
financial troubles, and they couldn't provide for
me on Christmas. It was a hard thing to come to

grips with, but it was also a wake-up call in that it helped me grow up quicker than others. I knew the hard times like I knew the back of my hand, and I had realized at a very young age that life ain't all peaches. There are times when you can barely survive. There are times when it seems that everything is falling down right in front of you, and there is nothing you can do about it. That's how I felt whenever I had to go to school.

When I looked up again at my parents, they both came over and gave me a hug and kiss and let me know how much they both loved me. That actually felt greater than anything at the moment because I was getting what I really wanted, and that was love. Nothing could have taken away from that special moment. And that's when I thought to myself what I originally believed to be a terrible Christmas actually turned out to be a very memorable one. We had a good dinner, and we sat around watching television, just accepting what was going on in our lives at the moment.

From that day on, Christmas wasn't about getting presents no more; it wasn't about getting ahead in the game; it wasn't about outdoing your neighbor with lights and decorations. It was about spending time with those you love and adore. That's what I always cherished most about the holiday

season. The time you get to spend with those loved ones and, of course, a good meal to go along with everything never hurt at all.

That Christmas vacation was nearing its end, and I, for once, was actually enjoying myself. My friend, Bobby, and I would end up hanging out the rest of the vacation by trading baseball cards and riding our bikes around. It was cold outside, but we didn't care; we just enjoyed the freedom of not having any homework and not dealing with those wonderful cherubs at school, telling us how different and worthless we really were.

The break from school was going so well that I ended up hanging out with these two guys from school that never gave me trouble, but that I wasn't very close to. We decided to ride our bikes through town and head to the local Ames store located at the ass end of Milton. Upon arriving there, the one guy by the name of Billy gave us a heads-up that he planned on shoplifting a few items while he was there. Trying to look cool, I said that was cool and that we should go in and get it over with. Billy went his own way for awhile, picking up whatever it is that he was after while Zachary and I decided to stick close together because we weren't used to the skills of stealing things.

Feeling a little weary, I started to walk a little faster than the average person up and down the aisle. Zach had wanted to steal some batteries for reasons till this day are still unknown. Maybe he just wanted to look cool in Billy's eyes by taking something that didn't belong to him. But the problem with that is Zach didn't have what it took to be entirely dishonest so he started to sweat and pace back and forth up and down the aisle trying to figure out if anyone was watching him. Seeing how nervous he was, I offered to steal the batteries for him and then give them to him when we left so that Billy believed that Zach indeed took it.

Looking around to see if I was under anyone's radar, I lifted the AA Energizer batteries into my pocket and then motioned Zach to follow me. We exited the store before Billy, giving him the notice that it was time to go. Right before Billy came out, I gave Zach the batteries and didn't think anything about it. There must have been something suspicious about the way we were in that store because a security guard was right on our tail. Looking back on the whole ordeal, it was as obvious as the nose on my face to an adult what we were up to in that store.

Luck must have been on our side then because the security guard searched us and found the

stolen items on Billy and Zach and made no quips about me leaving them behind. I still never found out what their punishment was, but I was happier than hell that I got away with something. That was definitely a much appreciated warm feeling. In the nick of time, I landed those batteries in Zachary's pocket and got away scott-free.

Obviously, we three never spent much time together after that incident, but that was quite fine with me. The Christmas vacation was now over with, and it was time for me to return back to school. When I stepped foot back into the hallways, the sneers started up as quickly as they began. From down the hall, I could hear the words being yelled out, "Hey shit pants! You need to shit yourself again? I brought a pair of your mother's underwear if you need to wear them, you worthless piece of shit!"

This quickly frightened me. I don't know why, but I was scared of confrontation and knew that if I began to fight someone again, that I would get no help while the other guy would have at least two more clowns on his side. My steps became quicker and quicker as the screams got louder and louder. Thankfully, in the last second, I got to my classroom and didn't have to deal with what was going to happen if that guy had caught up to me.

Actually, the only thing that I had wondered about was whether or not the girl in the hallway still remembered the incident. Every time I thought about her my heart would begin to beat louder and louder. It was as though she consumed all of my time while I was in school. Often times I'd imagine myself being a professional basketball player and having all of those girls love me and guys wanting to be my best friend and spend all of their time with me. That was one hell of a fantasy for me. I bet she would like me then. She would probably tell all of her friends about me and how smooth I was. Of course, this was just a fantasy that only danced in my head. I wouldn't dare allow anyone to know of it.

When I spotted her in the hallway, I tried to work up every bit of courage to say hi. My throat was running dry. My lips were constantly being licked to keep from drying out also. I began to clear my throat and puff out my chest to hopefully impress her just a little bit. I finally made eye contact with her, and before I had the chance to actually speak, she looked over to her friend and started laughing while possessing an obvious pointing to her suggesting that I was the center of humiliation. It stung a little bit, but it was something that I was

pretty much used to by then so I chalked it up as another day on earth.

Chapter 4
Dirty Deeds Done Dirt Cheap

There's so much in life one regrets. There are so many trials and tears one goes through. Pain is a wound that bleeds constant agony, which isn't seen by the human eye. It's like a disease that goes undetected, and it oddly enough is the number one killer amongst human civilization. The circle and journey in life never ends until the day your heart stops beating. You never know what is valuable and irreplaceable in your life until it disappears and you wonder how you ever got by without it.

The fact of the matter is we are not alone on earth; there are many things that go on around us every second that would astonish us. What lies beneath us isn't explainable and maybe even incomprehendable. What's real and what is a fabrication of the mind is only determined by the effectiveness of the situation. Beware as you begin to dive further into this story, which is twisted, gut wrenching, and beautiful in the eye of the magician who knows his magic and ways are clouded by the world's ignorance. Although there is a way to win

your destination, you just need to pay close attention to your own voice in your head and listen to their hidden meanings because there is a place that holds the key to it all, and whoever finds it has the ability to open all with his mind and health.

What I am about to explain shortly is pure truth and reality. I guess through everything there was a reason, a reason I can't define, a reason I may never be able to find. I know a person must fight for everything he believes in because when the moment comes that he doesn't, he just ends up another follower, and he ultimately gives up his right to his decisions because everything in his judgment becomes dictated and controlled by people who don't know how to run their own lives. It's easy for Satan to dominate and run your life when you give up that personal strength. Every decision one makes leads to his life's journey. Hard times may either break or make you. Remember, you can only please yourself first because if you can't please yourself, you will never be able to please anyone else. There is no debate whether or not there is a God. There is a God, but God doesn't determine whether you end up in Heaven or Hell. You are the only one that determines that. No matter what predicament you ever find yourself in, you have a choice, and

that choice may be the first to many wise or self-destructing ways.

Taking life and its wonder and joys for granted may be the most ignorant thing one can do to himself. The one you love and cherish will move on someday. Expecting that tomorrow will always be there for a better life is just another strategy by Satan to rob you of your life. Never take for granted those in your life and those who care and love you. Things come just as quickly as they go. Satan can make a person die long before he is six feet under. When his presence lives in your mind, escaping and becoming free seems like such an impossible task. And that's a mind frame he needs you to be in.

It was a sunny afternoon in the middle of summer that I'll never forget. My friends and I were outside playing basketball when a man decided to approach us. He slowly walked up and asked how we were doing. Being nine years old meant not having that initial instinct that screamed run away. He was a nice man at first, holding a conversation with us about anything that we found interesting. I guess it was his way of trying to earn our trust. My friends weren't as trusting as I initially was. This I would later find out would be a major problem for me.

61

This man said his name was John and that he was a professor at Bucknell University. This peaked our interest just a little bit because we lived in Bucknell View Manor Court, and as a way to make us feel better about living in a trailer park, we thought we were connected to the university. Obviously, we knew this was nothing but a lie, but sometimes a lie helps you get through some of the rough times.

After several attempts at trying to get a decent conversation going, he finally came out and asked if anyone was interested in making a little extra money during the summer. No one was jumping at the opportunity, so I spoke out saying that I'd like to earn some money so I could buy some baseball cards and gum. Seeming happy that someone took him up on his offer, he said that he would show up on Saturday to pick me up so I could get started on my job.

The feeling of having something to do during the summer and having money sparked my interest. I thought finally I would be able to get some of the things that I had wanted without depending on my parents to get it for me. I spent the next few days thinking about my first job. It would be a chance for me to branch out and get a head start on the summer and also beyond getting the trivial things I wanted.

Maybe I could get some nice clothing to go along with the upcoming school year. That entertained my mind for awhile and gave me some hope that I previously did not have, at least not to the point that I could excited about.

The professor arrived at my house early in the morning, and I hopped into his fancy car. He had a keen smile on his face. This was a smile that at the time I didn't find peculiar, but it was one that, after years of questioning everything about myself, I remembered like it was yesterday. Perhaps this was someone that didn't think I was worthless and could become something in this life. The feelings were nice for awhile.

We arrived at the university, and as we got to his office, he gave me a list of chores that he needed done. They consisted of dusting, moving chairs and desks around, and rearranging books. I thought to myself how cool it was to actually have a job and how proud my parents would be of me. But, for some reason, they never seemed to show any interest in it. This didn't cross my mind until years later. I wish my parents would have stepped in and investigated this man before they let him drive me off into his car only to have my entire life rearranged.

For those first two weeks things were going as smooth as possible. I was getting my pay and starting to buy some of those things that I had mentioned before. All of sudden, events started taking a much different approach to the situations. The moment that changed everything had arrived.

As I was cleaning through his office, I felt the presence of someone right behind me. It was the professor nonetheless, and I wasn't surprised to see him there. Actually, I was relieved at first because I figured it was another individual showing up to start some trouble with me. These days I wish it *was* another person coming up from behind me.

After standing there a little bit, I felt something grab a hold of me. Fearing what I originally thought, I looked down and saw an older man's hand wrapped around my crotch. It was indeed the Bucknell professor. Standing there, my heart began a rapid beat that wouldn't stop. The sweat was forming all around my forehead and swimming down my face. His grip began to get a little tighter, and my penis started to get hard. He had this smile on his face, and he didn't say anything. John just kept moving his hand around on my crotch and getting a drastic feel of my dick and balls. Those few minutes seemed to have lasted an hour.

During this time, he started to speak in a low firm voice saying, "Norman, this ain't no big deal, you know."

The strange compulsion in my pants scared me as I didn't know what was going on with my penis. The professor started making low and long moans whenever he would put his hands on my penis. On his face possessed a pleasurable look that made my stomach turn.

At the conclusion of all of this, he told me my work for the day was over with, and he proceeded to pay me. This time he had given me a little more money than usual. When I returned home, I couldn't wrap my mind around what had occurred. Maybe it wasn't anything unusual I thought. Could all adult-child relationships be like this? So I lay down to sleep that night with a confused feeling in my stomach. When most people say they are confused about something, they truly don't understand the meaning of that word. My mind couldn't comprehend if what I was dealing with was right or wrong. I had never before had any sexual feeling towards another man, and I didn't have any feeling towards the professor, but something about having my cock being rubbed for the very first time enlightened me. It gave a tingling

sensation throughout my body and made me feel really good.

Even though in my mind I didn't like or understand what was going on, the same couldn't have been said with what was going on in my pants. I decided the best way to deal with this situation was to do what I had been doing the past two years, and that was putting a Metallica record on. This time it was my all time favorite record, *Ride the Lightning.*

The next day I decided it was best for me to go outside and practice on my jump shot. While making several attempts to perfect it, maybe even good enough to make the team, the professor once again pulled into the trailer court. As I walked over to his window, he rolled it down, asking if I was busy for the day. Hesitantly, I said no, and he asked if I'd be interested in coming down to the office to do some extra cleaning for a few more dollars. Initially, I said yes because the money once again could come in handy and get me some more candy and baseball cards.

Upon arriving to his office, he decided it was best for him to close the door and get right down to business. "Norman, he said in that gross deep voice with his hand placed directly on my knee, "you should understand something, son. I'm paying you

for your services around the office and sometimes that requires a little relaxation on my part."

Not quite understanding what he was saying, I just stood there nervously and agreed upon what he was saying. He then looked directly into my eyes and asked me what I thought about taking a nap with him but playing some games in the bed first. Once again, not understanding what he was referring to, only being nine years old, I agreed. In my mind, I was being paid a handsome amount of money by each meeting, and I started to think I was doing a really good job and that I was being rewarded for it.

The sexual encounters started to become more and more severe as the professor was getting more and more confident on what he could get away with. The fact that I had no one in my life that was looking out for me and that I let him know my school status was enough for him to know how to manipulate the situation. Professor John knew that he had on his hands an abandoned kid with no social life, and he could do whatever his perverted little mind could conjure up.

The next meeting with him would become something that I could never get out of my mind. Every time I close my eyes at night I start to see the whole ordeal going down, and it makes me literally

vomit. The vision of his mature penis touching me and lying warm and hard on my skin makes me wonder whether or not I ever had control over the situation. The professor started to breathe heavily into my ear, instructing me to bend over and understand what was happening was of my own doing and not his. He began to drop to his knees and unbutton my pants, managing to pull them down all the way to my ankles.

Then he began to take his fingertip and rub it back and forth on my penis until it became rock solid. Taking soft breaths on my dick, he began to remove his tongue from his mouth and gently use the tip of his tongue to touch the head of my dick. This caused me to jerk quickly back and forth and create quick sighs that I didn't understand or want to understand. Getting back on his knees, he pulled down his pants and showed me his penis. Taking my hand he used it to rub back and forth on his penis until moments later it was as hard as mine.

"Norman," he said, "this may hurt at first, but this will begin to feel better than what you have ever felt. Trust me, kid, I've done this before, and I know what I am doing."

Scared half to death, I whispered, "okay sir."

"That's right, son, call me sir," he said in a desperate horny voice. He then slowly but steadily began to slide his penis into my ass, causing me a great deal of pain. At first I yelled out, but he scolded me for this and made me be quiet, even threatened me if I yelled again. This was due to him not wanting any other people to hearing what was occurring. The feeling of his cock inside of me almost felt like a big sharp knife being drawn in and out of me. It was a sensation that felt like nothing I had ever before witnessed.

What does this mean? Am I gay? Like I mentioned before, I had never had any sexual feelings towards another man, but something about these experiences felt good in a sexual way but hurt tremendously in a physical sense.

I once begged him to stop, but he was too far gone in the act to stop. He said he did this because he needed to punish me for the things I have done. The professor made me believe that what was happening to me was my fault and that I called for it.

On top of everything that was happening in my life, this only made me feel worse than I already had. He would say things like, *if you weren't such a fucking reject, maybe you would come around more often*, doing what he could to entice me to come

around more often, and it started to work on me.

Almost every time we got together, he would demand me to pull my pants down for him. Sitting there in his computer chair, I would slowly pull down my pants while looking him dead in the eye with a mere smirk at times. He would stare at me with those red glaring eyes and start to put his hand down in his pants to make sure his erection was alive and well. He would then make me get on my knees and undue his pants so that he could stand over me and look down while I was doing this. It made me feel really cheap, but I couldn't figure out why. I was just a little kid, and I couldn't figure out if what I was doing what normal or not. Every time that I showed up to his place to have some type of homosexual adventure, I would feel really scared to the point where I would walk into the restroom and vomit. This, however, never stopped the professor from doing what he wanted to do.

After a month slowly passed, the professor found it necessary for me to experiment with shoving my new erection into his ass. He said it was only fair that I ram it up his ass after he did it for me for so long. I didn't know how to say no or how to get help at the time because my life was a whirlwind of misadventures and misunderstandings.

My parents weren't an active part in my life at this point, and I wondered if they would even care at all if they found out. I tried, on numerous occasions, to reach out to them but wouldn't get anywhere. My father was someone that I could never figure out too much. He was a man of very few words and never gave me any sense of direction.

The man would spend most of his nights cuddling up with a six pack or getting dressed in a peculiar way to head out for the evening. My mother was someone that I loved more than anything, but I was always scared to come to her in moments of desperation. I was always afraid that even she would look down upon me during this entire process.

People have a way of thinking innocence is something that only lasts awhile in their lives. Innocence is such a precious thing that once it is gone, you can never get it back. The feeling of that first kiss is one you will never forget. The feeling of that first love in your heart is so precious and rewarding. You don't know it when it happens because you are so wrapped up in the pain and confusion of losing what you love all so much. As adults, we become so lost and disillusioned that we cannot possibly find our way through the human jungle.

Those childhood moments are some of the most life-changing experiences you can come across, ever. The adult life is something we idolize during our childhood years, yet when we finally reach that point, we realize how hurtful and devastating those years can be. That's when everyone becomes fake and takes their side with people that don't understand them. We think if we conform to something that is popular, it will somehow save us from our disjointed points of views and ways. Why can't we as a society just be real? Above and beyond anything else, I wish we all could just be real and not spend precious moments dying and trying to please someone or something that will never quite understand us.

It all seems like a cloud of confusion for me anymore. What should I do, dear Lord? This lifestyle makes me want to take a gun, shove it in my mouth, and blow my mother fucking head off. Please help me. I'm fucking dying, and I can't take it anymore. This world is too cruel and misunderstanding for me to live in anymore. GOD. GOD. GOD. Take me from this hell that I stand in on a daily basis. Do you realize just how haunting my life has become?

The professor decided that on a holy Sunday afternoon, he would stop by my house and pick me up. As I got into his car again, he had the radio

playing, and it was Rick Springfield's *Jessie's Girl* being played. I could see in an instant the sexual arousal in his mind and eyes. I felt so scared and timid that I began to shit myself again.

The professor noticed the smell and asked in his professional tone, "What the fuck is that nasty fucking smell?" Looking over at me he said, "Norman, did you shit yourself?"

I replied, "yes, sir."

This propelled him to pull over to the side of the road, not too far away from my house, into the wooded area.

John told me to continue to keep walking back into the wooded area until he found it necessary to stop. The walk continued for about a mile into the woods until he motioned for me to stop and stand still. When he caught up to me, he said he was going to punish me for shitting myself. This meant he was going to have his lovely way with me.

When he pulled down my pants there was shit all over. It was running down my leg without any resistance.

The look that appeared on his face was mixed with disgust and sexual arousal. "Norman, he said, "just stand still, and this will all be gone in a minute. Just relax, kid; it will be all right very soon."

Once again, he managed to rub his sharp tongue up and down on my penis while I shivered in fear, wanting him to stop. He gradually started to glide his finger on the head of my dick and kept whispering to my penis like it could hear him. This is when he started to run his nose up and down on my balls while keeping his tongue planted firmly on my cock. This made me unload my cum very quick and hard. I couldn't help but to make drastic loud noises while having this mind blowing orgasm. The feeling of having my dick being played with felt really nice, but I hated it because it wasn't the person doing it that I wanted. He would love it beyond explanation when he would bring me to the orgasmic stage.

"Yeah, that's good, boy. Yeah, that's good, boy," he'd whisper during the process. It scared the living hell out of me every time this would happen.

What exactly did this mean for me? I thought. Was I gay? The one thought that kept coming back into my mind was the one of that girl from the hallway that saw me at what I thought was my most vulnerable moment. Do girls do this with men? Did other men enjoy the sensation of their cock's being played with and sucked?

It was one thing when he would play with my penis, but when he started sucking it, it became a different animal. It was as though he was truly trying to swallow my penis. He would make these loud and feminine types of noises whenever he sucked on my cock. It resembled a little whimper that echoed in my mind. I couldn't, no matter what, get that sound out of my mind. He'd say things like, 'This, you know, Norm...this is your own fault. You basically make me do this to you. Do you understand?' Always feeling a nervous wreck and scared, I'd just shake my head and agree with him.

Back home things weren't getting any better. My parents started to drift farther and farther away from each other. I couldn't figure out why or how this happened. Did I do something, I often times thought. Did they love me? Am I just another person in a long line of failures? When I would awake for school, I'd just see my mother sitting there in front of the television set with that blank stare on her face. It was as though nothing could disturb that facial expression or feeling. She was a woman stuck in her own ways of thinking and didn't take too kindly of others' opinions or ideas.

I know my mother wasn't the best person in the world, and I knew that my mother wasn't the best mother in the world, but you see, people,

that didn't kill me. I loved her more than I have ever loved anyone in my life. People just like to sit around in their little groups while they have a few beers and drug themselves with those pills that are nothing but heroin made in a factory. They think that they know a person to the point of judging, but what they don't realize is their sick and twisted ways of dealing with their own pain. It makes it much easier for them to point the finger and not deal with what they know is corrupt and disgusting. If they would spend their time examining their own fucking lives, maybe they would see the disgust and horrifying moments that make up their day instead of focusing on people like me because it is a much easier goal to accomplish.

It is so hypercritical for others to waste their precious time examining others' faults and short comings. They don't see the obvious that stands right in front of them like their overweight kids that are often times bastards. At least I had my father in my life. Those crooked little fingers point in a crooked way at people.

I guess society needs people like me to get through the day. What would ever happen to this world if there wasn't a person like me to get kicked in the face by words and fists on a regular basis. Every now and then I start to develop this

crazy kind of laughter. The laughter is one of those moments where I take a step back and look at the world and understand that everyone is fucking out of their mind except me. The society in little central Pennsylvania is crowded by corrupt people running our school systems and laws. They don't give a fuck about the kid that is losing control of his life. They don't care about the man struggling to make ends meet. It is just a little game to them that doesn't matter until one of their own falls to the wayside. Then again, they would just push that person to the side and act like they were never a part of their own little click. Yeah, that is just what those sick minded mother fuckers would do.

The professor would decide that alcohol would be something to ease the mood. I thought to myself it was harmless until it would get me to the point where I couldn't make any decent decisions. Not that I had conquered the basics of making good decisions before, but this would make it even tougher. Every time the professor would pour me a shot, I'd get more and more fucked up. Sometimes I'd black out and wake up with my asshole throbbing in some of the worse pain you could ever imagine. Other times I would think about the girls that I'd never get the chance to go out on dates with. They didn't care about me. I was just another dirt bag

in their minds that couldn't ever live up to their standards of living. I guess after awhile, I learned to accept that fact. What I couldn't accept was the constant anal raping that was going on every time I'd pass out drunk. My life was beyond spiraling out of control. It was like I was the only one on earth that possessed these problems.

I never met anyone like me. The uniqueness that lay inside of my soul was something that no one gathered in a short amount of time but me. I knew basically from the beginning of my life that I wasn't normal. I wasn't like the Jimmy or Susie Q down the road. I was either a few bricks short of a load, or I was so real from the beginning that it frightened people. Whatever it was, I was alone, purely alone, and it hurt like you wouldn't believe.

I didn't share with my friends about the rapings or molestations that were occurring in my life. I was too terrified that they wouldn't understand. And you know what? They wouldn't have understood. No one could have possibly understood what the hell I was going through during those moments. You know what it's like to be a kid and have a man ram his penis into your anus? It feels painful and uncomfortable. The best part about him shoving his cock into my ass was when he would finally cum in my ass. Then at least

it wouldn't be so rough and uncomfortable. It was wet and smooth then, and I learned to complain about that feeling after awhile. It wasn't a big deal anymore for that to happen to me.

Few people understand what it is like to be vulnerable to an older professor of Bucknell by being at his mercy. Did he know that what he was doing to me would affect the rest of my life? Didn't you understand I was dying little by little every time I would get raped and touched? Why did you do this to me? What did I do to deserve this my Lord; help me again. I feel like my skin is peeling, and my eyes are watering so fast that they can't sit still in my mind. Life almost seems like it doesn't exist.

People walking around and around don't seem to have a sense of direction as to what and where they are heading. We just crawl and crawl on our fighting knees on a day-to-day basis, hoping to find a cause to our means. We don't understand the marks we are leaving behind in this world anymore. It is as though we don't have eyes that can clearly see past anything that isn't laid down right in front of us. Is that a scary notion to believe in or what? Is that something we should wake up and fear on a daily basis or something that we should just ignore and pretend like it ain't happening? I guess that last

decision has always been our best bet. Yeah, I guess that is our best option and outcome because it is the most easiest thing to pull off. Am I angry? No. Just a little upset and angry at society for not taking responsibility in the way that America always has or at least the way we have always been taught it has.

The days of insanity kept happening. One of the scariest moments came when he decided to give me a handful of pills. Apparently, these were pills that were designed to help with his heart. Taking the handful of pills into my mouth, and I immediately began to feel a sense of dizziness and lack of concentration like I had never witnessed before. The room started to spin, and the floor started to move rapidly, too quickly for my feet. My head hit the ground really hard, and I was about to pass out, he gave me a shot of whiskey, which made me feel sicker than I had ever felt in my entire life. What was happening to my mind and body, I thought. Was this a natural feeling or one of those feelings that you become used to when you get older? All of a sudden the lights in the room started to flicker on and off, and my mind was racing at a speed faster than lightning. The next thing I knew I was crashing face first on the ground unconscious.

When I had awoken, my head was spinning

at an uncontrollable rate, and my heart was running at an alarming speed. Looking for a glass of water, I couldn't manage to get myself off of the ground. Out of nowhere, this older man pinned me down for good on the ground, and I was greeted with a large penis being jammed into my young asshole. It hurt beyond repair. The medication and whiskey that I had taken had taken over my mind, and I couldn't manage to scream or cry for help. It was just this old penis being rammed in and out of my ass, and I couldn't handle it anymore. I could hear the man that was raping me yell out how nice and smooth my ass felt on his old long dick.

He said that it was a fantasy come true. My body had never felt that much pain in my entire life and I couldn't understand why I couldn't speak out. For whatever reason, those men gave me those pills, and they took control of my body like you wouldn't believe. They left me paralyzed all over. Not one physical feeling was felt amongst my body except for the cock being jammed in and out of me. This fellow was finally done when he came about two or three times in me.

Unfortunately, the next two men didn't recognize the pain I was in, or maybe it turned them on. Either way, they managed to ass rape me even more, and it left me weaving in and out of

consciousness. I could almost swear that during one of those moments, I could see Jesus Christ's face looking me dead in the eye with a terrifying look that he could only give to a child that was being homosexually raped by a class or distinguished men. Jesus' eyes looked desperate and hurtful. My response was a simple plea to get me out of this mess. Get me out of this fucked up situation. Please, Jesus, do for me what you can because I just can't take it anymore. Please, oh please, I kept reciting in my mind. His visual presence kept fading in and out until it was no more. I just don't understand I thought. Isn't Jesus supposed to be there for the downtrodden and less fortunate?

That didn't happen for me though. The pain and agony just was something I guess I'd have to live up to. I didn't understand why, but I did. When the third man decided to take his cock and rub it up and down on my smooth young back I began to puke a little bit from my mouth.

He said, "Shut the fuck up, kid, and let me do what I came here to do."

Feeling absolutely terrified, I did what he told me to do. I turned over on my back and sucked his penis dry.

He kept repeating the words, "That's fucking right, kid, that's fucking right." It almost

felt like a newborn sucking on his mother's nipple. I didn't want to do it, I swear, but I had no choice. It was that or get the shit beat out of me and get raped anyway. Actually, now that I think about it, either way I was losing, and there was no use in me fighting it because it was going to happen anyway. I don't think this is what Jesus had in mind when he turned those tables over in the downtown street of those crooked misfortunate people.

The worse thing or best thing happened when that man was making me go down on his penis. I began to shit myself again. I could almost feel a fart coming on when all of sudden the shit started to drain out of my ass crack and run all over my body. Is this what you wanted God? A young confused kid shitting himself while he is sucking cock and or being ass raped? I couldn't pull myself away from the situation. It was the only time in my life where I was being accepted. What has happened to me dear Lord? My entire body was feeling like a hundred year old man. I was beyond worn out, and there was nothing for me to do anymore but to lie down and take it.

My life didn't possess the right friends to understand what I was going through, and my parents once again were so far removed from this incident that it scared me because I just wanted my

father to step in and end this shit. Why couldn't he just stand up and be a man and demand what was going on in my life to be stopped? Is that such a hard thing to comply with? Please, Dad, just come through for me just once in my life. Show me that you still care about me instead of your unusual weekends and alcohol. I'm dying for your affection; can't you see? Please save me. Don't you understand that you are my savior. You are the one that can turn this entire ordeal around for me if you just step in and try to help me. One of these days I will be a reflection of you. Do you understand I'm an only child, and you are the only one that can pull me out of this fucked up situation?

Please, Dad, notice my fear and uneasiness, and come to my rescue. Notice that I am a child in need of love and understanding. This ain't no cheap country fair scheme, man; it is me, Norman Jr. Help me please. This dinner you are providing isn't filling up my stomach, and I just can't handle it anymore. Will someone please rescue me? Will someone please rescue me? God, will you please rescue me?

Chapter 5
The Thing That Should Not Be

"Know you what it is to be a child? It is to be something very different from the man of today. It is to have a spirit yet streaming from the waters of baptism; it is to believe in love, to believe in loveliness, to believe in belief; it is to be so little that the elves can reach to whisper in your ear; it is to turn pumpkins into coaches, and mice into horses, lowness into loftiness, and nothing into everything, for each child has its fairy godmother in its own soul." -Francis Thompson-

The days of pure innocence to me were all but over. In my mind, I couldn't grasp what it meant to have something that wasn't corrupt or disjointed in some way. I began to understand that to "fit in" required giving a part of yourself up to an idea that didn't have you in its plans to begin with. To me, that meant going out of my way to please some kids that in hindsight never wanted me to be part of their schemes unless it meant benefiting them in some positive way.

So the days and hours rolled around to where I was walking into the nearest mall and stealing clothes and the latest hottest items for people. The

strange thing about that was I was good at it. It meant nothing to me to steal something that wasn't mine. The world had made me already into something that wasn't mine so in a way of responding to the mess that was my life, I had no complaints when it came to stealing from these places of business.

In one incident that keeps popping up in my mind there was the time I ran into the Lycoming mall and decided to grab that latest Michael Jordan shoes available. The kid I was with was named Timothy. He was this student of average height and a little underweight with bags consistently under his eyes. My so-called friend, Timothy, wanted those Jordan shoes more than anything, and he knew that someone of my social position couldn't begin to afford them. With his smooth talking and quick thinking, he managed to get the wheels in my brain to start turning, and within minutes, I was sold on stealing those shoes for him.

So the circus parade began, and I was roaming around the store for quite sometime. No one, for some reason, expected that I was anyone to be alarmed of. Then I found the exact pair of sneakers that he had wanted, and my mind was made up that they were going to be mine, I mean Timothy's, before the day had ended.

I waited for a good two more hours until the mall made its little announcement about the store closing down in a matter of moments. This caused the employees to begin to take certain sales back into the break room and other employees to clock out ten minutes earlier than they should. The moment was there for the pickings. I grabbed the shoes, and in a calm manner, I walked myself out of the store without so much as a whisper said about it.

Finally, the event of that day was over with, and Timothy had a new pair of Jordan's to wear to school. Doing this for him made me feel like I was finally in the new cool crowd, that everyone had finally forgotten about my shitting incident. Unfortunately for me, that wasn't the case. When Tim got back to school, he made it clear that he had worked enough jobs during the summer to get the money to pay for the sneakers.

This made me feel like I couldn't take it anymore. Tim went on to explain that he and his friends had a wonderful time at the mall hitting on women and getting the shoes that he wanted.

Was I completely losing my mind, I began to think. This mother fucking cunt decided that he was going to take the credit for this incident where I laid everything on the line. He left me in the dust for

everyone to continue picking on me. That feeling was so cold and lost that I didn't know how quite to respond to it. I felt like no one had ever loved me. Do you know what that feels like, that feeling that no one thinks you are worth anything but a kick in the face? Till this day, I remember lying in bed, crying myself to sleep.

Some days the tears were even too warm to make me go to sleep. I'd pray to the Lord above that someone would see the child hiding way inside the soon to be adult. No one understands the impact of hurting another individual. The actions and opinions we create often times are nothing purely what our parents thought of certain people growing up. They didn't take into consideration the pain and agony one can go through. They never witnessed the tears and heartache that someone spent while they were lying in their bed. The tears that stained and soaked through their pillow cases were just a dime a fucking dozen for many.

Why should that bother me, I often times thought. Will there be anyone there for me, when the time comes, that I need more than ever? The daunting realization of no one in this world taking the time out to look inside of my fucking heart and know what I feel and what is going on is hard and incomprehendible. How I made it this far was the

latest task that was lying in the realms of my mind. I decided to write a letter to God in hopes he would hear my latest story.

Dear God, What else have I left to say to you? These days are getting almost too dark too see that I don't know where I am going or even thinking. What should I do with all of these feelings that are lodged inside of me? They keep ramming their ugly head in front of me, and they don't understand the pain and agony they have on me. Do you know that I am consistently being raped by a professor that is respected in his environment? It makes me wonder whether or not I am to blame for all of this. Did I bring all of this attention to myself? Am I the freak that everyone keeps saying I am? Please, God, make this shit all end for me. I can't fucking take it anymore. You have no idea what it is doing to me.

It is almost like I have a side of me that I don't even fucking recognize. I'm not the person the world thinks I am. If someone would just give me the chance, she'd see that I am just a person trying to make it in this century of lost souls. People think that I am such a lost soul that has no sense of direction. I'm not this worthless piece of shit that everyone thinks that I am. Will you please pull me out of this horrible nightmare? There are times like these where I am crawling up in a tiny ball in my

bedroom, begging for you to come through for me. I want to take my life, but no one even sees the pain that is lying inside of me. Everyone is looking at the school dance that is coming up, but I'll be the kid standing there dressed up as nice as can be, standing all alone.

When all of those kids are dancing and enjoying the beat, I'll be the child stuck in an old man's mind, dying just to survive the latest scene. But somehow I know there is something that is better than what I have been living. Do you understand what I mean, God? Is that something you can really connect with?

My letters to God weren't something that I was unfamiliar with because they were a ritual that I had for quite some time. People didn't understand the importance of this for me. It was the only thing I could do to keep my patience and understanding with the world. People, for whatever reason, didn't like me, and after a long time of knowing and dealing with this, I finally accepted what was my fate.

I am one of those people that didn't have a chance in the popular crowd. Hell, I didn't even have a chance contending in the crowd that was surrounded by dorks, but I had enough dorks to hang out with that were never lonely to begin with.

I didn't even fit into *this* crowd. I was just a loner. That's how I viewed it. In some strange way, that didn't bother me because it was something that I held sacred inside of my soul. Who was anyone to question whether I was normal or someone that needed help beyond measure? It didn't matter to me at that point because I was so tired of being lonely. No one quite understands this because it is something that no one wants to come to grips with.

It is one of those things where someone starts to believe that theres no such thing as a perfect place for him. And you know what? That is okay because we all don't belong somewhere without our fellow man. Who says that exact moment where all is right and wrong with the world, and who tells you who to decide to spend time with? We all think that life is one big bubble waiting to burst. The truth is we decide our own fate.

After all of this stress, I couldn't help but go to the professor since at least he showed me some sort of attention. When I finally got to his office, he was already there with his pants halfway down to his knees.

Taking a few steps into his nice little office, he asked me to take a seat while he took care of the rest. "Norman, you don't have to do any work today,

The world was almost like a complete state and country away. I didn't know what to think when all that I knew was crashing down upon me. How could I? I didn't know any better, and still no one was paying close attention to my life. Does anyone know the exact feeling of losing everything that you thought was true and glorious? My honest innocence was beyond gone, and there was nothing I could do about it. The days of insanity just kept pushing on like it was almost supposed to be.

What made me even more uneasy and confused was that the molestations were becoming even more hectic than they were in the beginning. My ability of sucking dick had become almost pro-fessional. I knew how to do that as well as anything before. John had become someone that made me trust him no matter what. That smile he would put on his face was beyond inappropriate. His third tooth in from the left side was always slightly inward than the others and had a strange yellow tint to it. Whenever that tooth would show in a smile wide enough, I knew that trouble was in store for me. I'd usually have to get down on my knees and call him sir just long enough for him to get an erection and start making his legs move in a provocative manner.

When this started to happen, he would make sounds that would come along as deep yelps for help, even though that wasn't what he was going for. That was just his way of saying that he was having the time of his life. What was it about me that made him so fucking horny? His orgasm noise always sounded like something from a movie that was a mix between a horror movie and bad b-rated porno.

The feeling of sucking his dick was probably the most disgusting thing that I have ever had to witness in my entire life. It was almost like second nature by the time I began to be good at it. He would have this strange way of making me feel dirty and good at the same time. It was almost obvious that he knew whatever he was making me do to him was wrong because he had a way of always making me believe what was happening what the result of my own ignorance. Back then I didn't know the meaning and understanding of sticking up for whatever you believe in so I just went along with whatever was happening. I mean, no one else was paying this type of attention to me so at least I was becoming something I had always dreamed of. And that was a person that was desired. Did this make me wrong? Am I actually a homosexual?

My mind just kept scrambling on to the point to where I didn't have a clue as to what I was or who I was. Maybe this was always what was supposed to be. Some days I'd just lie in my bed and question whether what I was doing was ethical or not. The trailer park I was living in only possessed the qualities of people that made them only sensible to converse with the people that they thought were them, which made me even more in trouble because I wasn't even good enough for *them*? What the hell has happened to me, dear Lord? Sometimes when I think of all the wrong I've done, I can't believe it is me that I am talking about. You know what I mean? It is something that makes you colder inside than what you think you already are. Please, God, forgive me.

Deep into the end of the school year brought me across another person that I wasn't too fond of meeting. This time it was Jason. He was this kid of average height and weight but had a reputation that no one could put his finger ready on the trigger. For whatever reason, he didn't like me no matter what I did. He always treated me like a third class citizen that didn't have a chance of making it in the least possible way.

People in school would look at Jason like he was some type of rock star because he was such a

great skate boarder. Something about that kept the girls going crazy. It was as though they thought he was the answer to their prayers because he could use a damn skateboard well. Oh, and he didn't respect any authority at all, making him a tough guy figure.

One day when we were almost done eating lunch, he decided that it would be funny to push me right into the trash cans. I responded back by calling him an asshole that didn't have a clue as to what it took to make it in this world. What I forget in my moment of anger was the craziness that Jason possessed. He wasn't like the rest of us in that he looked forward to trouble and wanted it nonetheless. He would have done anything it took to have the chance of hurting someone and adding to his punk ass reputation. So it was no surprise when he took that step forward and called me out.

I'll never forget his words as they rang in my ear that entire day. "Hey Norman, you shit pants piece of garbage, how would you like for me to just beat the shit out of you instead of you just sitting alone in the class and letting it happen?"

This caused an uproar of rude laughter amongst the kids in the cafeteria. Unfortunately for me that didn't connect with what I was hoping would happen. His eyes began to turn a dark shade

of red, and his fists were clenching each other to the point where I thought that vein in his neck was going to pop.

Jason made it clear that he was going to hurt me in ways I never could imagine. Little did he know about the trauma I had gone through in the past couple of months. But, that didn't matter because I was scared of him. He wasn't a very big person, like I said, but he was someone that I just couldn't imagine winning in a fight against. When everyone around us was chanting for us to start to fight, I began to sweat profusely. This was apparent to him because that evil smile on his face began to grow larger and larger.

Finally, he started to speak because he looked me dead in the eye and said, "Gundrum, I will see you after school, and when I do, I'm going to stab you to death." In this he took out his switchblade knife to show me he wasn't fooling around.

My nerves were beginning to tighten, and I was finding it harder and harder to breathe. What was it about me that made people want to continue to fuck with me? What did I do to this asshole that made him want to actually hurt me? The only thing I did was stand up for myself, and God only knows that that doesn't happen very often. Maybe he thought I was disrespecting him because I

finally did stand up and not take the usual trash talk from people. In his mind I bet he believed that I was challenging him. The hardest guy in school, and I am the one that has to make him think I was challenging him. Why me, I often times thought, why the hell me?

Sitting in class during that time, I began to feel my insides rumble and get that feeling of taking a shit. Luckily, this time I made my way into the bathroom and didn't shit myself again. The thought of being beat up and possibly stabbed by this guy made my insides frightened beyond measure. The only thought in my mind was to get the hell out of that school before the final bell rang so I could escape my unfortunate fate.

Almost twenty minutes before that final bell rang, I grabbed my belongings and cut class to avoid a possible beating and stabbing. Till this day I didn't know whether or not he would have actually done anything, but I sure as hell didn't want to find out the hard way. That fear stuck with me for quite some time. That feeling of looking over your shoulder wherever you go in case someone is waiting for you around the corner isn't any way to live your life. I kept a keen eye out for Jason for quite awhile. He never decided to bother me after that day for whatever reason; I don't know.

Maybe he never showed up to that wondrous spot we were supposed to meet or maybe someone told him something about me that made him too scared to show up. No matter what the case, I was just so happy that it didn't end up in me being hurt over absolutely nothing.

During this time, the professor started to come around a little more than usual, which meant he was horny and couldn't find any other little boys to take advantage of. When John would pick me up, he would make me believe that I was actually going to be doing some work instead of sexual favors between his friends and him. The list would usually include putting the right files in alphabetical order and not letting past or future students have access to his personal files and schemes. Fortunately for him, this would never happen with a student. And it really shouldn't have because he was much more interested in my penis more than he was anyone else's at the time.

When we finally arrived back at his place, he immediately demanded me to pull my pants down and start to gently touch my penis. This was something that hadn't quite started out like this before, and it made me feel very awkward. I gingerly took my first two fingers on the left and rubbed them back and forth on my cock. 'Yeah,

Yeah, that is what I want to see,' the professor kept expressing. The next thing I knew was that my dick was as hard as Japanese arithmetic, and the professor had wanted to finish things off.

A few seconds later, he managed to get on his knees and slowly suck the tip of my penis. This made me very aroused, and I didn't know why. I liked my dick being played with because the orgasm would provide me with a very good relaxed feeling, and for a few seconds during that time, it was as though nothing existed. The hard time and the bad breaks I had in life were just a distant memory whenever I would blow my load all over the professor's smiling face or all inside his asshole. Fucking in the asshole is never a pleasant experience. It takes so much tedious effort to actually get the penis inside the real asshole and not hurt the other person by doing it.

The professor must have loved my dick that was hard and dry because he would purposely yell out in pleasure every time he realized what was going on. I could see the vein in my penis throb up and down every time it got really hard. It would allow me a sense of pleasure that I had never previously known before. How could this be, I often thought to myself. Something about having an orgasm really drove me wild. Feelings of all those juices flow

right out of my penis just fascinated me, I guess. It meant I was getting something taken care of that needed quick attention.

Going to the professor was the only thing that I had basically known. As traumatizing as it was at times, it was also the only place where I could get any attention. But the worst part about it all was every time I had received attention, it was always in the worst possible form. From being consistently raped in the ass to sucking on an adult man's penis to being bullied at school, I often times contemplated suicide.

How wonderful it would be just to escape this constant hell that I live in. To just take a gun to my head and end it all would be the final blow to a life that was treating me more than unkind. I often times wondered if anyone would actually miss me at all. Is there anyone out there in the world that ever thought of me on a daily basis just long enough to take the time to reach out to me? Maybe so or maybe, not but regardless, no one ever did. I just kind of took every hit in the face as a stepping stone to my future dreams. It's a wonder what one can accomplish when he is lying down to sleep, and the moments of the day start to ramble on and on in his head.

I thought that I would end up being one of those hopeful stories that you see where a musician or artist that got picked on in school finally had there shining moment where they could be on top for just a little while. Long enough to see the other side of the spectrum and not one that made you feel worthless. People think its fine to treat someone like they are garbage or to throw their problems in their face as though that pain and agony will go away. It doesn't go away it just manifests itself into a monster. A monster that will eat you alive many times over and you don't have the slightest clue that it is happening.

You begin to coast through life like nothing is happening to you, that all the memories and thoughts of the past weren't really a part of you. You pretend to notice that nothing has changed. All of the friends and places you've been start to fall to the wayside. Until one day, you stare into the mirror, and you see someone looking back at you that you don't recognize.

Deep down inside you know that it is indeed you staring back through, but your heart won't accept it. Your mind finds a way to quickly accept that it is you in the mirror, but your heart takes a little bit more time. The heart is something that isn't easily fooled. The heart knows the past and

the present so damn well that it fucking scares the living shit out of you. The evidence surrounds us all the time...from the way we feel when we haven't seen a person in awhile and finally running across his face, to smelling the first breath of spring each season. They all tie into one another in some fashion. We just fail to realize it because it is something that frightens us, and the world we live in doesn't like to admit to being frightened.

We all just make believe that everything is all right so that the true feelings don't have to come to the surface any sooner than they have to. This makes our coping skills a little dull, but we don't mind. It's the present that matters and not the future. Our emotions become so cloudy with who we *are* and who we were *trying* to be or become. The human psyche tells us to manifest our thoughts into trivial things because that pleasure is like a high. So all in all you could say my mind was a little on the left field side instead of the center where it seemed everyone else was.

When I finally awoke from my what seemed like a month long sleep, I started to feel that perhaps something was going to come my way. I didn't know exactly what, but my hopes and prayers were getting a lot stronger than before.

Arriving to school almost ten minutes late, I managed to get in my seat without the teacher noticing, which was no big surprise. Sitting next to me was a rare but good friend by the name of Nathaniel. Nathaniel was just this plain kid that didn't make too much noise and most of the time just kept to himself. When I noticed he was trying to get my attention, I leaned over to his side of the desk and asked what was up. Looking rather excited, he mentioned that he was having a few people over that night and wanted to know if I wanted to stop by and hang out.

Of course, I thought in my mind, but not wanting to sound to anxious, I just gradually accepted his offer without much excitement running through me. Nathan explained that his parents were to be gone for much of the evening so we all could stay up late without worrying about any parents getting in the way of our fun. Happy as can be, I spent the entire day at school, anticipating that night. In my mind I just kept wondering about all the fun stuff that we were going to do that night. I supposed we would play some Super Mario Brothers and perhaps a few good games of basketball and probably end the night with a good scary movie...all of the things I would fantasize about as a kid desperately seeking friends.

Finally, the school day was over with, and I raced home to get ready for the night. I started to pack some clothes and extra underwear in case my problem would arise yet again. Thankfully, it was only a few hours until I got to Nathan's house and the partying would start to take place.

When I got to his house, there was a bunch of people our age and a little bit older. Most of the kids I knew, and some of them I didn't. What surprised me most of all was that no one was taking notice that the kid who shit himself was there. It was almost like a dream come true for me, I thought. Walking throughout the house, I finally reached Nathan, and he seemed to have a little bit of a buzz as he introduced me to his sister, Marie. Marie was quite a pretty girl with wavy brown hair, a crooked but decent smile, and a cute little laugh. She reached out her hand and said it is a pleasure meeting you. I just smiled and replied with the same answer.

Surprisingly enough, that was the first time anyone had ever told me that it was actually a pleasure meeting me. It was kind of a nice feeling I felt. Later on that night we ordered a bunch of pizzas and began to devour them. Marie put a few slices on the plate and wanted to know if I wanted to go upstairs and play some Uno with her and eat the pizza. Not thinking anything about it, I gladly

accepted and made my way into her room.

When we got in there, she said that it would be a lot more fun if we made the game of Uno a little more interesting. I didn't see any harm in making the game a little bit more interesting so I once again accepted and followed her rules. After all, I was used to following others' leads by now. She went on to explain that whoever couldn't match the card with the same color had to take off a piece of clothing. At first I started to feel uncomfortable because of my previous encounters with taking my clothes off. It must have been quite obvious because she could see the sweat start to beat down on my face. Feeling nervous and uneasy, I once again accepted the latest change in the game.

"Don't feel awkward, Norman," she said, "it is very natural for us to do this. My parents do it all the time," she softly giggled to herself. The rest of my nervousness came because I had never previously kissed another girl before or even touched one for that matter.

The game got off to a good start with both of us sharing the duties of taking our clothing off. After about fifteen minutes passed, she said that the game was taking too long and I should just do to her what I came there to do. At first I was a little confused, but Marie managed to clear things up for

me really quick by slowly giving me a kiss on the lips. My very first one! I thought, this feels a lot better than the professor's lips. Marie's lips were very gently and soft. They were also plump and made me feel something I had never felt before.

Then she slowly began to unbutton my pants and giggle very sexy as she did it. Looking at me dead in the eyes, she said, "Norman, isn't there anything you would like to do?"

"Uh, uh yeah, I guess," I nervously responded. Taking my hand, I pulled up her shirt and started to kiss up and down on her chest. I specifically remember her nipples being very warm and entertaining. Slowly, I made my way down to her crotch as she did the same to me. I noticed she had a thin vagina and was wet. Finally I began to slide my penis in and out of her vagina. Being my first time, it kept coming out, but after a few attempts, it stuck in there.

She was going at it like it wasn't her first time at all. I appreciated the eagerness and the experience from someone that wasn't an old man and who didn't force it upon me. It was by far the greatest thing I had ever witnessed or done. Our sexual encounter lasted but all of three minutes, but it was three minutes that made me a man for the first time ever. I was just eleven years old while she

was a cougar being thirteen years old. She treated me like a man, and she made me feel like one. I remember afterwards she said that we should do it again sometime. Before she could barely finish I replied with an eager yes.

As Nathan's parents arrived home and started yelling at him for all of the people being there without their permission, I thought it best to leave with the memories of the night. Sex isn't too bad, I thought...at least doing it with the right person for once.

Getting back home, I climbed into my bed and just drifted away again into no man's land, the place that was sacred and no one could hurt me. That place was my own mind. Things had to begin to get better, I once again said to myself before my eyes closed to sleep.

Chapter 6
Disposable Heroes

There are times some moments between a father and son help shape exactly whom an individual becomes. My father was, for the most part, always good to me. We didn't always see eye to eye but that was okay because I didn't see eye to eye with anyone. Our talks though often times would be brief and would carry a lot of significance for me. I always looked up to my father for being a man that was there to raise his family and get through the tough times. He might not have been the richest man in the world, and he might not have been the greatest father or husband around, but I knew he loved me, and sometimes in life that is the only thing that really matters. Just knowing someone does actually love you can carry a lot of weight when you need it to.

I began to speak to my father much more than I had in previous years and started to learn things about the man behind the television stare. During one of our talks, he asked me if I ever had the desire to take a vehicle out on the open road

and just get away from the hustle and bustle of the world and just become one-on-one with myself. Absolutely, I quickly responded. Little did he know how much I craved that exact feeling on a day-to-day basis. Day after day I'd lie in my own bed and just want the ability to get away from it all, perhaps leave everything behind and just go away for good and never look back. Yeah, that would be the perfect getaway.

'Norman, he would say, 'grab the car keys, I'm teaching you how to drive today.' Getting that anxious feeling that a kid gets when he knows something great is about to happen, I rushed over to the kitchen table and grabbed the keys, waiting for my old man and I to hit the open road. We headed on out to the Milton Elementary school to get down the basics of the game. Even though I despised the sight of that building, I felt a warm response to it this time because my father was with me. A kid always desires things out of life anyone couldn't just give. There are moments and emotions only certain people can spark in another, and this was one of the incidents where my father was the only one that could come through and make me feel safe.

I guess the biggest thing that kept me from going after what I wanted in life was fear. How do

you classify fear, I always wondered to myself. It is something that has the ability to rip you into tiny little pieces and make you feel like an incompetent little child whenever it pleases. Some people say that it keeps you in line while others say it completely handicaps you from ever accomplishing your goals and desires. Fear can be both, I guess. It is our way for people to keep themselves in denial while they think it keeps them in honesty. It doesn't do that for us unfortunately; it just eats away at our soul to the point where we just think that what we are doing is normal.

I don't remember the time and place where I began to deal with fear in a positive way, but I do know it wasn't when I was spiraling out of control in ways I could never imagine.

My father finally got out of the driver's seat and let me climb on over to get behind the wheel. My heart was racing a million times per hour, and the sweat was creating beads across my forehead. Graciously putting my hands on the wheel and turning the key to get the car started, I could feel the vibes of the engine roaring through my bones.

After putting the car in drive, I started to go around the block and get the feel for everything. It was almost surreal how it felt being behind the wheel, just having the freedom of getting out

whenever you wanted to without the worry of how you are going to do it. Also, getting my first driving lesson at the age of twelve put me in a position to be a little ahead in the game. It was those moments spent with my father that I cherished the most. There are certain emotions and feelings that a child will go through during his childhood years. It is essentially the pieces of the puzzle that make up who we are.

We made a few trips around the block before we decided to head out to the Montandon baseball fields. This is where I wound up getting the most experience driving wise and understanding when to know when to get out of the driver's position. Sitting behind the wheel made me feel like a man. And this was just the second time in my life where something made me feel like I was a man, the first being when Marie made my dick wet, and now this time, cruising around Montandon with people I knew seeing me take charge of the situation. Everything was going quite smooth until I accidently backed into a telephone pole. You see, I thought I had the vehicle in drive, but instead I put it in reverse, and the damn car backed right up into that pole. Fearing for my life that my dad was going to scream at me, he was instead very calm and gave me encouragement just by the soothing

sounds of his voice saying, 'Next time, Norm, just look down to what shift you are putting it in so you know for sure what you got in store for you.' This made me feel like number one again. Here we were, my father and I, sitting together, learning how to drive with not the slightest worry in the world for me. Some people ask a lot of questions about my father, but I can tell you that he loved me and didn't kick me when I was down. I hope you are reading this, Dad, and know that I love you very much.

Some of the loneliest times in my entire life were during the times when I didn't feel the connection with my parents and peers. It was almost like when I woke up in the morning and looked into the mirror. I'd say this couldn't be my life. You ever get that feeling during those lonesome times? How could this be my life? The days are filled with poetic sorrow, and the nights are a bottle full of hopeless tears surrounding my every move. Sometimes it was as though it just hurt to move a muscle. Every muscle represented a painful memory or situation yet to occur.

When I'd walk through those hallways and hear the banter that followed my every step and move it created a neverending hole in the pit of my heart and soul. My heart and soul were never on the same page because they would be played with

on a constant level. From the professor picking me up at the trailer courts on a consistent basis to lick and suck my cock, from the kids out on the playground never letting me join in on any of the kickball tournaments or flag football, to the final sound of heartbreak when arriving home and seeing my parents not speaking one word to each another. How is that a way of living? That is purely a way of dying, in my opinion.

I always thought that there was a difference between someone being comfortable in his skin to a person waking up to die. And I was right as far as I could tell. I'd envy the kids in school that could get any girl and friend they mother fucking wanted. Fuck you. Fuck you. And you know what? Fuck you too. The world did nothing for me on a consistent level other than shit in my face. Oh yeah, I can almost hear the jokes now from my classmates: "Well, at least we didn't shit in our pants" or "Hey Norman, you ever think about just ending your pathetic piece of shit life?" Of course, these phrases would be followed by laughter spreading throughout the room. It was these moments that made me feel like I was going insane. Who I was? I honestly didn't even know anymore, and the worst part was I don't know if I ever even had the slightest clue as to who I ever was.

This time upon walking home from school, the professor met me halfway and took me to his office. I didn't immediately get a chance to come into his office because he had meetings with students lined up. How any of them didn't recognize the strange fact that I was there still to this day bewilders me. Maybe they thought I was one of his kids or possibly a grandkid at that point. Regardless, they never even stopped to ask me, which is no surprise really. I was used to being ignored or bullied.

When all of the students were finally out of his office, he slowly but firmly called me in. Taking a look around at the scenery of the office, I knew that he had other kids in there to fuck because things were different from the time I stepped in there this time compared to the rest. The professor asked me to take a seat in front of his desk.

Then he began to display a little role-playing as he started to speak in a way that was in tone with one of his students. "I didn't want to give you a failing grade on the last test, but I had no choice. You have been a very naughty student. I think you really need to start showing up for class, son."

All of a sudden, I could feel my heart start to race once more, and the beating pace never ended. He had this devilish look in his eye like he knew exactly what was going to happen in that instant.

For some unknown reason, my breaths and whimpers were getting louder and louder.

He firmly said, "Now fucking relax. This isn't going to take forever." Then he continued on with his evil smiling and once again unbuttoned my pants and began to rub his nose on my dick before making me stand up, only to bend over the desk. "Now this might hurt at first," he said while making me stand there completely naked in pure fear. This is when he jammed his penis up my ass and began penetrating to the point where I thought the old man was going to have a heart attack. The pain that I felt inside was unbearable, a lot more so than any other previous time spent with him doing these disastrous scenes. Not only was he raw and hard, but he went into me dry as a bone. Or boner if you are reading this and finding it humorous and delighting.

When it was finally over, he didn't even have the decency to give me a ride back home. It was more on the lines of okay, I'm done with you, and it is time for you to leave, and leave me the fuck alone, kid. This to me didn't matter because I was so relieved that it was actually over with. After leaving his office and stumbling my way back home, the pain I felt inside my ass was so severe that I started shitting myself uncontrollably. The feces just kept on rolling out and out and I couldn't

figure out how to stop. The feeling it gave me was very horrendous. I felt so ashamed and terrible about myself and the situation that I lay down in the woods for a few hours and cried myself to sleep. The tears rolling down my face seemed like I was standing in the midst of a water fall. I couldn't understand or figure out why this was happening to me. Once again, why me, I thought. What am I doing wrong, God, that this must be cast down upon me? 'Why, oh why,' I continuously screamed out. That didn't matter because there was no one around to give me comfort and to answer that question.

My life had taken one hell of a roller coaster ride in twelve years. I almost laughed to myself thinking about it. As soon as I got back into the house, my mother was making me dinner. She didn't even take notice of my once again shit filled pants, so I just threw them in the dirty hamper and continued along my way. Feeling as dirty as I did, I thought it best to jump in the shower and get the rest of the shit off of me. The rest of the night just went along in the same vein they all did, so I closed my eyes and went to sleep. But for some reason this time I had a dream that was unlike anything that I had ever dreamed before.

In my dream I was standing in a meadow surrounded by nothing but the clothes on my back.

For the longest time I felt like I had no sense of where I was or what I was doing there. Everything just seemed so peaceful in a manner that only someone with the experiences I had could understand. After what seemed an eternity, I looked up, and there was this man. The man didn't look like anyone I had ever encountered before so I stood there gazing at this man with pure magic. He stood a solid six feet tall and looked as though he was around one hundred seventy pounds. This older gentleman wore a calm and confident smile, almost like the professor, only his seemed in a manner that said he wasn't going to harm me but had a proposition that could possibly bring me some decent fortune.

The clouds and sky started to join together in a sort of fluorescent color, and it made everything seem too surreal. I couldn't figure out exactly how to put my finger on it, but it was almost like the path to heaven was lying down right before me. My eyes were spread wide open, and they were gazed with imperial light like no one had ever witnessed. I couldn't believe my sight. It was as though there was an angel standing right over my bedside. The angel didn't talk or do anything of the sort but just hung right over me as if to say I need to reconsider my ways. At that moment, it didn't dawn on me just how crucial a moment like this could actually be.

These days when I look back on such times, it brings a tear to my eye that I can't even begin to describe. Often times I'll sit here in this what seems a padded prison cell and just ponder about all of the times I had growing up where I could have taken care of the situation I was in instead of wishing like hell it would resolve itself. Too often I sit and wonder what all my life could have possessed. I guess looking back on it all, it really doesn't matter after all of these years. But it was dreams like those that kept me desiring so much more while accepting so little.

School though would seem to get just a little bit better. It was around this time that I was introduced to the librarian, Dean Slusser, and his assistant, Nellie Koch. These two would prove to be crucial to my life and understandings. Mr. Slusser was always sympathetic to me after a hard day of being bullied and picked on. He and Mrs. Koch would often times stand up for me and offer valuable advice. I just wish nowadays I could have listened to what they were saying instead of letting it go in one ear and out the other.

Nellie had this strange way of understanding an individual on his own level. She wasn't out there to judge or correct anyone; she was a kind soul that would take time out of her own day just to listen

to whatever was going on in my mind. Though I don't believe she knew exactly where I was coming from, she was always sticking up for the underdog in the bottom of it all. She could sense the hurt and urgency in my eyes that had been hidden away from the rest of society. My comfort level in all of this was starting to get better and better. I'd get used to going down to the library and listen to her talk about her dog and how to ignore the kids that were making a career out of hurting me. The woman possessed a sense of understanding and wisdom that is rarely found in people. One of my fondest moments growing up would be of her talking to me on how people only say to you what they are inferior to themselves. Some of her sayings to me went straight over my head like the one "they'd complain if they got hung by a new rope" and the ever so famous "half of his lies aren't true." It was comments like these that made me laugh hysterically and yet at the same time understand as to what she was trying to convey.

Often times Dean Slusser would make me feel right at home by going over my studies with me and helping me get by the classes I was taking. There was something about these two people that really stuck out to me. They were offering me all of this help yet expecting nothing in return. I couldn't

understand any of this really. No one before had ever welcomed me with open arms without expecting me to go beyond my means to help them. Sometimes lying here at nights reminiscing, I would wonder if people could truly understand how much those two were there for me. It felt very nice not to be judged and looked down upon by somebody, especially someone that was much older than me. Their genuine care and understanding kept me a free man longer than what I had honestly hoped for. I remember distinctively that every kid that went down to Mrs. Koch would get understanding and hope that wasn't portrayed to them by any of their teachers and counselors. Kids had a way of knowing who was actually looking out for them and who was just trying to make a paycheck. Mrs. Koch wasn't any of those people to me or to a lot of other kids that were struggling on a day-to-day basis.

Another one of the teachers that would help me extraordinarily was Mrs. Beaver. She would take kids like me to get shoes that we couldn't afford. It was those people that made me feel like I really belonged in society. It was those kinds of teachers that made me feel like I wasn't a waste of time. It didn't matter what they did or didn't think about us because when the time came to be what they

should, they were always there. Because of them, I was wearing the latest Michael Jordan shoes out there, and no one was questioning why. The feeling of someone there loving me because she wanted to made me fee like I was the only one out there who mattered. To me, I always wanted to be that guy at the high school dance that was making other people jealous. If you ever decide to read this, Mrs. Beaver, I hope you know just exactly what you meant to me. You were great and made me feel like a person instead of a number. Thank you.

I still remember those days while I was still in Milton where Mr. Slusser would take me to those church youth groups and let me hear their religious talks on the world and the society we lived in. I bet all of those people never expected what was to come of my life. Sometimes, looking back at those people, I would laugh and laugh hard, and other times like now, as we speak, I'd hang my head in terrible sorrow not understanding what made me be the person I was, even though it was clear to everyone around me. I'm just a person, I would often times think to myself. What did the world expect of me? You can only push a person so far until he finally snaps on you.

Did this mother fucking world think that I was going to go unscathed through all of this

bullshit? Fuck you, Milton. Fuck you, society. I hope you all understand exactly what the pain and agony was for me. Until you have actually been bullied and misunderstood, then you have no idea what it is like to be an underdog. Just remember, you highly prestigious people out there; your kid could end up being the next one that is picked on and bullied to death. Just remember this: the apple doesn't fall too far away from the tree.

People like me had to stick together because we were a rare breed, and it didn't take long for someone to spot us out and start to hurt us with their words or fists. Sometimes I wish I just would have stuck up for myself and punched one of those punks square in the nose. Maybe I thought I wouldn't have ended up in the position I am in now. But regardless, it is those thoughts that don't mean anything anymore.

Once again, it was the end of the day, and I was heading back home. I still remember the little old black bible that we had in our house. It was a little beat up around the corners and front cover, plus the pages were a little yellow also. Something inside of me said to pick it up and give it a good read. There were parts of the bible that I was finding very rewarding. That night before I lay down to sleep, I got down on my knees and prayed to God that he

would help me find a way to break away from this mess. Please Lord, just stand by me tomorrow and guide me day-to-day. It was this following passage that I kept by my side. I made a note of this and kept it in my pocket wherever I went for the next few months.

1. And seeing the multitudes, He went up onto the mountain. He teaches us not to do anything ostentatiously. For when He is about to teach, He goes up onto the mountain, thus instructing us also when we would teach, to depart from the bustle in the city. And when He had sat down, His disciples came to Him. The multitude comes for the miracles, but the disciples come for the teachings. So when He has finished the miracles and healed their bodies, then He heals their souls as well, that we may learn that He is the Creator of both souls and bodies.

2. And He opened His mouth, and taught them, saying. He taught not only His disciples, but the multitude as well. He begins with the beatitudes, "Blessed are they," just as David began the Psalms with the beatitude, "Blessed is the man."

3. Blessed are the poor in spirit, for theirs is the kingdom of heaven. First He lays down humility as a foundation. Since Adam fell through pride, Christ

raises us up by humility; for Adam had aspired to become God. The "poor in spirit" are those whose pride is crushed and who are contrite in soul.

4. Blessed are they that mourn, for they shall be comforted. "Blessed are they that mourn" for their sins, not for things of this life. Christ said, "They that mourn," that is, they that are mourning incessantly and not just one time; and not only for our own sins, but for those of our neighbor. "They shall be comforted" both in this life, for he who mourns for his sin rejoices spiritually, and even more so in the next life.

5. Blessed are the meek, for they shall inherit the earth. Some say that the "earth" is the spiritual earth, that is, heaven. But understand it to mean this earth as well. Since the meek are thought to be those who are despised and deprived of wealth, Christ says that it is the meek, rather, who possess everything. The meek are not those who never get angry at all, for such people are unfeeling and apathetic. Rather, the meek are those who possess the capacity for anger but control it, and become angry only when it is necessary.

6. Blessed are they who hunger and thirst after righteousness, for they shall be filled. Since He is

about to speak about almsgiving, He first shows that one must pursue righteousness, and not give alms from what has been acquired by theft and extortion. And one must avidly practice righteousness, for this is what it means to "hunger and thirst." Since it is the greedy who are thought to be well off and satisfied, Jesus says that it is rather the righteous who shall be filled, even here in this life, for what is theirs they possess with surety.

7. Blessed are the merciful, for they shall obtain mercy. Not only with money does one show mercy in almsgiving, but also with words. And should you have nothing at all to give, show mercy with tears of compassion. "They shall obtain mercy" even here in this life from men; for if he who showed mercy yesterday should be in want today, he will obtain mercy from all. And in the next life, how much more mercy shall he obtain from God?

8. Blessed are the pure in heart, for they shall see God. There are many who are not rapacious and greedy, but are generous in almsgiving, yet they fornicate and commit other uncleanliness. Christ commands, therefore, that along with the other virtues we should also be pure, that is, chaste and temperate, not only in the body, but in the heart as well. Without holiness no one will see the Lord. Just

as a mirror will reflect images only if it is clean, so also only a pure soul admits the vision of God and the understanding of the Scriptures.

9. Blessed are the peacemakers, for they shall be called sons of God. "The peacemakers" are not only those who are themselves peaceable with all, but also those who reconcile others who are at odds. "The peacemakers" are also those who by their teaching convert the enemies of God. Just as the Only-begotten Son reconciled us to God when we were His enemies, so too are the "peacemakers" "sons of God."

10. Blessed are they that are persecuted for righteousness' sake, for theirs is the kingdom of heaven. It. is not only the martyrs who are persecuted; many others are persecuted as well, for helping those who have been wronged, and simply for every virtue which they possess. For "righteousness" means every virtue. Thieves and murderers are also persecuted, but they are not blessed.

11. Blessed are ye, when men shall revile you and persecute you. He addresses the apostles directly, showing that it is especially the mark of a teacher to be reviled. And shall say all manner of evil against

you falsely, for my sake. It is not simply he that is reviled who is blessed, but when he is reviled for Christ's sake, and falsely. If these two conditions are lacking, he is a wretch, as he has been a cause of temptation to many.

12. Rejoice and be exceeding glad, for great is your reward in heaven. Of the others whom He has said are blessed, He does not speak of a great reward. But here He does, to show that to patiently endure reviling is a great and most difficult thing; so difficult that there have been many who have even hanged themselves to escape this trial. Even Job, who patiently endured his other trials, was troubled when his friends reviled him by saying that he was suffering for his sins. For so persecuted they the prophets which were before you. So that the apostles would not think that they would be persecuted for teaching something contrary to God, He exhorts them by saying, "Even the prophets before you were persecuted for the sake of virtue, and so you have the example of their sufferings to give you courage."

When the Earth and Mankind fall. My word will still live on forever. Amen

Many times being an only child had its benefits, I thought to myself. Whenever we had money, which wasn't all of the time, my parents made sure that I'd get my fair share in bubble gum and baseball cards. Every time this would happen, you could see the glee shining right off of my face. At least I didn't have to share any of the good with anyone, I thought. Often times I would use this excuse to make myself feel better about not having someone that I was related to relate with me and spend time with me during those harsh days at school and whenever the professor would decide to ride my dick as hard as a fucking horse.

Though there were times when I'd hope like hell that my mom and dad would have had another kid so I could at least have someone there with me. I would always wish that there would be an older sister so I could be cool and possibly date her friends. That way it could have potentially stopped the bullying that happened to me. Everyone seeing me date an older girl could have done wonders for me. What would my older sister look like, I also thought. Would she too be a member of society that was beaten down on a daily basis, or would she be a pretty girl that all of the boys would have died to just go out on a date with? I could have been her cute little brother when her friends came over, and

129

eventually I would have gotten older, and one of them would have wanted to date me. In my mind, I always played out the scenario where one of her hot looking friends would take notice of me as a man and tell me how attracted she was to me or something of that sort.

Or maybe I could have had a brother to spend time with, maybe someone who would want to go outside and play some basketball with, go girl chasing and fight off all of those bullies who thought they were so tough. Those assholes wouldn't have known who they were dealing with if I had a brother, and we both stuck side by side. These fantasies often times would haunt me because it would leave me hurting at the end because I didn't have any of those things in my life. I was just a person that wasn't making it the way that I had always desired. Teachers teach us all of the time to strive for our goals, and our parents always tell us we can be whatever we want to be when we grow up. This is so far out of reach as being true because society would never allow someone like me to actually become what I wanted to be. Why would they? Why should they? If I always look at myself as not being as good as those people, then maybe I'm just not. That's a horrible way of looking at yourself, isn't it? Oh well, I'd think maybe that is just what

dreams are for, nothing but the hope and thought of doing what you want to in life.

It was starting to get to the end of winter time, and the weather was giving us those teaser days. You know the kind where it gets really nice out for a day, then the next it goes right back to being a freezing hell hole. Yeah, those kinds of days are what I am talking about. My best friend, Bobby, and I were heading out to that skating rink located in Shamokin Dam. We were happier than hell the weekend had finally arrived, and we spent the entire ride up there talking about all of the pretty girls we would meet there. Maybe they would think we were these cool types of guys that were getting out of their hometown just to get away from all of the attention. Our minds were wandering a little too far out of reach for the both of us.

The line to get into the skating rink was much longer than any of us expected. So to pass the time along, we started to goof off just a little bit. This led to a few unpleasant situations for us. First, a few guys kept staring us down, and once again I thought trouble was on its way. I think that people targeted me because I was usually the tallest guy, and this made those people with short man syndrome feel much better about themselves. Rarely did I ever pick a fight with those losers because fighting was

something that I just wasn't too keen on doing. What pleasure could I have possibly gotten out of that, I thought. Then I took a look to the right of me, and Bobby was teasing these girls. His attitude was perverted, and it was starting to embarrass me. To make matters even worse, I was starting to like the girl standing right in front of me a lot more because she was just so gorgeous. She reminded me of the way *I* was because I could spot someone with that uneasy feeling a mile away, and this started to make my blood boil. 'Knock it the fuck off,' I kept saying to Bobby. This wasn't flowing through his mind the way that I thought it would so in a moment of panic and anger I reached back and punched him right in the face. This knocked him down, and he wouldn't think of getting back up to fight me or bother those girls again.

Everyone stood there and started to laugh. The girls had this sense of relief over them that made me feel good and proud, but that taunting laughter at Bobby made me feel like I was a few inches tall. Why did I have to hit the fucking kid, I kept asking myself. He was just trying to have some fun, and I let my own biases and anger get in the way and hit my best friend in the face. What the fuck was I thinking? I mean, the guy needed to stop all of the bullshit, but I could have handled it a lot better than

what I actually did. The few girls standing in front of us let me know that they were happy I took care of the situation. Still though, doing that to him only made him feel worse than he already did on a daily basis.

When we finally got into the skating rink, one of the girls came up to thank me for getting him to stop teasing them. She said she wasn't used to guys standing up for her and thought it was really sweet. She stood on her cute little tippy toes and gave me a kiss on the right cheek. Man that felt really nice, I thought. She had golden red hair and moved in such a sweet innocent way. My mind couldn't bear to get her out of it. What if she could possibly be the one person in the world that I was looking to save me?

During the rest of the time, I kept thinking about her, and she kept spotting me every single damn time I would look her way. Then all of a sudden, I could see her whispering to her friends, and the only thing she could have been talking about was me. I just knew it. During this time, I would also look over to Bobby and, to much of my surprise, he was having a decent time regardless. He didn't need me either. For the first time in his life that I took notice, he was enjoying himself and not giving a flying fuck whether I was with him

or not. This made my conscience feel much better. Knowing that he was doing well, helped urge on my feelings for this girl.

When she came over the next time, she introduced herself as Sara. Sara, I thought, what a gorgeous perfect name for a girl like that. This is when her friends started to scatter around the skating rink and give us a little bit of time to ourselves. She stood up again and whispered low in my ear to go out back with her. Feeling like this was going to lead up to something worth remembering, I followed her without any hesitation. When we got outside, she asked me if I would like to feel her up. Now I only had a slight view on how this was supposed to be done, and I took a chance on that anyway. Reaching my hand up her skirt, I could feel her slowly developing breasts and felt an emergence in my pants that I hadn't felt since Marie came along. Sara began to make moans, and this made me even more aroused than before. 'Fuck me Norm,' she started to say in a low but firm voice. That nervous feeling was coming over me again, and within no time, I had begun to slide my penis into her. It felt very nice and wet. The warmth of it made me blow my load at a record time. She didn't seem to mind though. Her eyes and facial expressions were as alert and satisfied as she wanted them to be.

Looking back on it now, she wasn't looking for a great long fuck, but instead something that would cure her teenage desires for a few moments. And a few moments is exactly what I gave her.

The rest of the night there wound up being pretty strong and good. Bobby and I were making up with one another over our incident, and it was time to go home. We both learned a couple of lessons there, which were to stick by your friends, and that women love it when you stick up for them. They appreciate the confidence and care you extend to them in times of danger. Whatever the case was, we had some of our best times at that rink, listening to the top forty and just skating our day away. That is what childhood should be about, I started to think. This is what makes me enjoy other peoples' lives and not criticize and hurt them.

Shane Hoffman

Chapter 7
I Am

I am. Now what the fuck does that even really mean? Is it a statement that leads to what we claim ourselves to be? I am. What am I? A boy or a man? A freak or a child?

Sometimes what is the most difficult thing in life is the ability to deal with yourself and the life you have lived or been thrown into. The corridors of my mind had led me to places I only feared or dreamed about. They were realms of society that didn't reflect anyone other than me.

Does it ever scare you what you know? I'm terrified at what I can do at times. In those desperate moments, human emotions are real. My emotions are occasionally beyond real and desperate. Everyone around me gives me that look like I am so different from them. Fuck all of those desperate attention-craving whores. One would think growing up in a small town would provide a person with the self-respect and safety that he craves, but instead it gives him a sense of being lost and a feeling of hopelessness. To me, watching those people

scrounge and scrounge around for the approval of the heartless bastards around them makes them as hopeless as the people whose attention they seek.

People hide behind a facade of who they are every single chance they get. They feel that if they do this, then the world will never see what lies within their own hearts. Isn't that the truth behind this all? People waking up on a day-to-day basis trying to figure out for the life of them who the fuck they really are. No one really knows these days. It is just a non revolving door of selfless, hopeless emotions being shadowed by fake smiles and drugs. That's the healthy way of dealing with things, don't you think?

Sometimes, when growing up, I would think that things would work themselves out. But they never did do that. They just kept piling on and on, and it got to a point where I couldn't handle it anymore. What is one supposed to do when he feels as though whatever he does is completely powerless? I used to watch the lonely faces pass me continuously through the hallways of the school and wonder if they had it as bad as me. I guess these days it doesn't matter because we all know how I ended up. It all adds up to nothing, in my opinion, short of confusion and hopelessness. The events in my life wouldn't help matters at all either,

especially when it involved me trying to live my life in an honest manner.

Well, it didn't take long for Bobby and I to find ourselves in a predicament when we decided to head down to the island for a day of fun. We both were down there exploring the trails, playing soccer, and throwing a little Frisbee from time to time. It all started out so innocent and free, but hasn't everything started out like that in one way or another?

I guess my worst mistake in all of this was when I let the professor know that I would be heading down to Milton Island that day. Apparently, it was a place where faggots met up and would have some special time with one another. To me, this was unchartered territory, and till this day, I wish it would have stayed that way. I could almost feel the unbearable pain wreak havoc in my insides and emotions. It was something that wasn't about to go away.

The prestigious man approached me in a calm and subtle kind of way. He said that he was one of the prime members of the church, and he would help me forget all of the sins and wrongs that were cast down upon me in my previous life. He made those words seem too real and believable that it made me want to listen to everything he had to

say. This man made it clear that whatever was about to happen to me was only understood in the eyes of God. When a man makes this kind of promise, you tend to believe him, especially when you've got nothing else to lose. The older gentleman would talk to me about God and assured me that what was going to happen was planned for me. So just like every kid that ran into a preacher that was supposed to be a man of God and trust him, I did exactly that.

Well, he guided me into those bathrooms that can barely hold five people and made his way onto me. The tears in my eyes started to form like rain in the clouds, and they broke out like a hurricane when he made me drop my pants. 'Please sir, please sir, don't do this to me,' I kept pleading with the man of God. He dropped his pants and with a beautiful grin slammed his penis right into my asshole. It hurt worse than ever before.

All of a sudden, I felt like vomiting beyond belief, as he kept screaming out bible verses like they were a way of making him feel better at what he was doing. I just kept yelling STOP over and over again. Please, God, make this stop. I repeated that phrase my entire life. The sensation of his penis into my anus was as painful as shoving a nail through your dick hole. My ass just felt like it was

about to fall out after all of this sexual abuse. He then started to yell at me like it was my fault once again. 'Shut the fuck up, you little snot. This is the most action you and your retarded friend will ever receive.' Those words ran inside my head for days, and now those days have turned into years.

When he was finished, he rubbed the rest of his sperm on the bathroom toilet. He then began to create a strange sexual moan whenever he would touch something that he knew that men had pissed or shit on. It was beyond horrifying.

Poor Bobby, poor Bobby, I continuously thought. What did he think about all of this? He was the one who managed to calm me down during the entire process. My trembling only increasingly got worse and worse. It almost got to the point where I thought I was going to die or shake in a death defying seizure. My eyes were focused on the sky. The movements and the shape of the clouds kept me mesmerized. The colors of the sky were turning from blue to green to a dark black. It was as though the heavens were watching every movement in that fiasco and in my life that I considered nothing but a joke.

Why would this happen to me? It must have been something that I was born with. That was the only explanation for all of this, I thought. The

broken heartedness was seeping through with every step I was now taking. The entire Milton school system was falling down on my shoulders, and the kids were only getting older and meaner as the time passed by. That scary look that I now own in my eye came from all of that. People, till this day, wonder how and why I ended up in the predicament that I was in. I've always answered that question with, *what would you do if this happened to you*? Of course, none of them had the brain power to process what I was saying so it just ended up going in one ear and out the other. The powerful stares and the threatening remarks started to play on my heart and soul after awhile. Maybe what they are saying is true, I would often times think. Am I the worthless piece of shit that everyone says I am, or am I just a product of what I was doing at that time?

Till this day it all has become a blur, something that I have only just began to understand. I don't believe people have any sense of understanding and realization of what human emotions can do to another person. We think that it is something that will just pass and, with time, get better. We all know that ain't the truth. Unfortunately.

By this time, I had already failed seventh grade for the first time, making the second go round not as pleasant as I had originally thought. In my

mind, I thought that maybe the kids coming up weren't keen to the notion of me getting picked on and wouldn't start that cycle all over again. This moment in my fantasy danced around the entire summer as I anticipated hopefully starting over in the same school with a different set of kids. The feeling of failing stung, but it didn't affect me to the point it did most others. I had learned to be accustomed to such moments so it was never a surprise when something wasn't going my way.

The teachers held their conferences and wanted to know why I couldn't do the work. Did it ever cross their mind that it's hard taking a test when someone is spitting at you or calling you every nasty thing imaginable? Or could it have been my anxiety kicking in, knowing that it was only a matter of time before I shit myself again? Many times I wondered if these people in the Milton school system knew or were just blind to the fact of how certain kids got treated. Regardless though, the river of emotions continued to drown me on a daily basis.

The first day finally came once again where I would take my usual self into that beautiful school and hope for the best. Upon sitting down in that class again, I already felt the stares. Apparently, the kids in the lower grades were much more social than I was and often times knew the other kids in the upper

grades. The old dirty looks returned, and the old life was once again in full swing for me. It wasn't a big deal, I thought to myself. I did everything I could to not cry in those moments. In my mind, I always told myself that I was a big boy and that it wasn't any big deal. It was those moments that hardened me but, at the same time, softened me.

On my way home from school, it was a bright sunny day, and the only thing I wanted to do was escape whatever was happening to me. I ran into one of my friends, Ricky. We had a small amount of weed and a can so we decided to make a bong out of it. Being this was the first time I ever smoked marijuana, I was hoping it would have a drastic effect on me. Instead it had a very dull effect on me. I've seen other people smoke weed and do drugs before, and it struck me as something that could take my issues away. It didn't do that for me, unfortunately. Well, I guess that was a fortunate thing in the long run. God only knows that a drug addiction was the last thing that I would need. In fact, if that drug would've felt good, it might have been the death of me. Perhaps in that moment, God was looking over me.

That school year continued along in its usual fashion. My unfortunate curse of shitting myself continued also. I used to feel so worthless every

single time that I tried to stop it and couldn't. That same question of 'why is this happening to me' used to run through my mind at an alarming speed of one million times per hour. How is this happening to me, God? That constant feeling of your feces coming through your own asshole and soaking through your pants was one of the most demeaning emotions a human could possibly experience.

What people don't see in me is that I have a passionate heart, one that loves and lives to be loved, even it if it is just for a little. I don't know why I care so much about others' perceptions of me. Maybe it is because I crave that attention in hopes that it will get me to where I need to be. Whenever I see a pretty girl from outside of my little old town of Milton, and she passes me a smile, it makes me feel as though I'm not the piece of shit that everyone claims me to be. It doesn't take much for another individual to bring my spirits up, but it takes a lot of abuse anymore to bring my spirits down.

As the school slowly but surely progressed, I had come to realize that my stay in Milton was almost over with for good. I entered that summer looking for something to keep my mind busy. Finally, I had rid myself of that college professor and didn't know exactly where to find my attention. No one had really shown me that kind of attention

before, but I didn't enjoy it at all because it came at the expense of my mental state and sexuality. It wasn't hard gearing up for a lonely summer, but something in my mind wasn't settling right. I hadn't talked to Bobby in a couple of days and was wondering if I had possibly done something that would have offended him in some way. I didn't let it possess too much of my time as I spent that summer drifting around and lying awake at night like I usually did.

Fortunately, and now after all of this time, I can say that my summer in Milton went by quickly, and now it was time for a new school year. This time Milton only meant being there for the very beginning before the staff and parents thought it would be best to move me to another school.

In my opinion, one of those incidents where I scared the school too much is when I was in my homemaker class, and we took a trip to the hospital. Once we arrived, the setting was your usual scene. There were the old sick people and the nurses rushing back and forth to their rooms and sitting at their cute little desks. Upon arriving to the section where God's gift of birth was happening, I heard a woman screaming. It scared the living shit out of me. What the fuck was happening, I thought. Is someone being murdered in there? I couldn't take

it anymore. The thought of a woman being in that much pain horrified me. My skin started to turn pure white, and it felt like the blood was draining right out of my soul. Please stop, I kept thinking to myself, please stop. Eventually it did, but it didn't keep me from vomiting and losing control there. I never knew that was how much I couldn't stand to see someone else in pure pain and agony, and to think it was all for another life to be born. I guess it is rather quite miraculous.

After that little incident, I began life in a new school, a system known as Sun-Vo Tech in Sunbury. I wanted so badly to fit and not be picked on, and that's exactly what happened. For once, I wasn't the bad kid or the guy that shit himself and got picked on. People were treating me like a guy without any real issues or problems. I began to see my talents flourish in ways I had only previously dreamed of.

I had three teachers at Sun-Vo Tech, even though I don't remember their names. I learned French and mechanical drafting. I went from F's to all B's and C's. There was this older couple who would come every day to see the class and would just be there to talk to us and help mentor us. The older guy taught me how to play chess. They were like another set of grandparents.

147

For the first time in my life I had actually felt like I belonged somewhere and with something. I used to go home every night and pray to God and thank Him that I found these people in my life. He had put them there for a reason. I thank him for my grades as well as my life and attitude changed. I started to feel loved, like I was a somebody instead of a nobody.

Do you know what it is like to look in the mirror and see someone you are truly proud of...to know that you aren't the worthless piece of shit that everyone says you are? That feeling got me through some dark nights and days. I just wanted to keep it real, and keep it real is exactly what I did. I have to say now that Sun-Vo Tech was one of the greatest things to have ever happened to me.

Unfortunately, that stay in Sunbury was one that wasn't meant to last. The following year I was placed back into Milton, and the trouble and bullying picked back up at full speed. The usual snares and remarks started to come back into full swing again. 'Hey, shit pants' was a term that had not long passed those senseless fucks' memories. All of the positive emotions and experiences that I had achieved were now slowly but steadily being flushed down the toilet for something that I couldn't once again control. These people really have it in

for me, I continued to think to myself. Their lives must have been pretty fucking miserable for them to continue, after all of that time, to tease me again. Maybe their daddy's were raping them, and their mommies were selling their bodies for drugs and money. Insensitive people kept running around in my mind and life. It wasn't too before I started acting out and getting in trouble again.

This time it started with me lifting up a girl's shirt to see those young beautiful titties. Those nipples had to be twice the size of an average woman's, and they sure did look nice to me. What I wasn't expecting from her and her capabilities was a good old fashioned ass beating. She managed to give a swift kick in the balls and then follow it up with a good right hook to my face. I admit it; I got my ass handed to me by a chick. How it happened, I still don't know, but it did. Like I said, that started this whole train a rolling.

The only thing that was going good for once was my draw of girls. Like I had mentioned before, I went out of town to get my fix in when it came to women. One girl that I considered a girlfriend was, in reality, nothing but a good time. Her name was Brandy. Brandy didn't let me go all the way with her, but she did let me do something that I had previously not experienced before. And that was the

sweet taste of going down on a girl's vagina. It might not have tasted like cherry pie like Warrant said, but it tasted the way a woman should. I always thought that the logical next step would have been to have sex, but apparently she was satisfied with having her cunt ate out. I can't complain though; it gave me an erection harder than Japanese arithmetic, and I later blew a load too.

Brandy thought it best to get rid of me after awhile. She must have found her night in shining tongue then because I hadn't heard from her since. I wasn't the best at it, but I gave it my all, and that didn't stop her from moaning the entire time.

But that little heartbreak led me to another girl that I still consider a beauty queen. She went by the name of Cindy B. She consisted of being very short with blonde hair and was built perfectly with nice breasts and butt. She also had a great personality. I used to smell her hair because it reminded me of the spring time.

We used to lie awake together and talk about what we thought happened to us when we die. I used to say, 'well we just go to sleep in heaven.' She would giggle and act as if I were completely wrong. That didn't bother me though; it was just nice to have someone there that wasn't treating me like a worthless piece of junk. Someone to hold onto and

tell her that I loved her was what counted. The only thing that I couldn't reveal was that I was sexually molested and a loser at my home school and town. I didn't want to drive away anymore people than I had already. So to stay on the safe side, I kept my mouth shut and acted as though everything was good. And good is how I wanted it to be. I got tired of all the bullshit that was going on in my life that I just wanted everyone to leave me the fuck alone for once.

My terrors were only starting to surface for a permanent time though. I continued to skip school and find other events that I thought were worth my time. In reality, it wasn't the best of decisions to cut class and hang out in Smoker's Alley. After a few more fights and arguments, I officially flunked out of Milton, and that would be the very last time that I would ever step foot into that school again. Bigger and harder things were on their way for me. Events and people at the time I couldn't change, but now, seeing things more clearly makes me realize that staying away would have saved my life. And maybe someone else's also.

Before we go through all of that, I must mention a few good/bad/ugly/terrible stories with you. Starting off, Cindy B. left me after getting a glimpse of what my life was like due to the

carelessness of a friend. Secondly, in a line of a million other things, was that my life was flashing before my eyes.

Chapter 8
Numb

In a world full of people, so many are bound to come across a few that are numb. That so was the case for myself, Bobby, Kenny, Ricky, and possibly Harry, most of the time. We felt like the characters straight out of the book, <u>The Outsiders</u>. We were the ones that were always hanging on in the outside, just creeping by slowly enough to get noticed.

Starting out our usual walk through town, Kenny mentioned that there was a basketball tournament going on at Lebanon College. We packed ourselves into Harry's car and headed out towards that school in hopes of winning that basketball tournament. When we arrived, we were all shocked by the amount of teams that had already signed up. It was clear that it was a three-on-three matchup that night, so we had to list Harry as an alternate since he was older.

In those days, I looked up to Harry for the fact that he was older and seemed to be what I wanted at that time. Everything between all of us

at those moments was cool and relaxed. Nothing seemed out of place and irregular then.

The tournament continued, and we started out by winning our first game, but that excitement started to die down quickly because we got our asses kicked. The rest of the teams were way out of our league, and we couldn't keep up. It didn't matter though because we all got out that day and managed to have the time our lives. I didn't care that we lost. Having friends meant something really special to me, even if it meant traveling out of town to go somewhere where I would lose anyway.

The ride home was filled with laughs and everyone telling their dirty little stories about the sexual experiences they had had. I didn't want anyone at that point to know what I had experienced so I kept a tight lip on everything. Having everyone know that kind of business would have made an already shaky situation even harder to deal with, and God only knew that I didn't need that.

Later that night, I decided it would be good to spend the night over at Kenny's place. We started out by continuing our stories about sex. My stories were on the line of getting my dick sucked and pounding a girl like a mallard duck. That always got a lot of laughs from them, and this made me feel like I was cool and popular. It wasn't so hard to

fabricate a lot of them because in reality we were all telling tall tales. Not one of us had actually made a girl squirt across the room seven feet, and neither of us had actually made a girl scream 'fuck me louder than a Metallica drum solo' either. But it was fun that we had these dirty stories to tell and got our kicks in based on these little white lies.

In the morning, we all decided to head out to Knoebels. This was something that we all looked forward to. Once we arrived, it was off to the races of eating as much funnel cake and riding the rides as much as we possibly could. Kenny, Ricky, and I would spend our time talking to as many girls as we could while trying to get their numbers. At times, we would succeed and get what we wanted, but all too often we got rejected.

The times we found what we wanted, we enjoyed partying a little bit with those girls, but nothing turned into any of us getting laid. Most of the time the one getting the number was none other than me. Kenny and Ricky often times would portray a smooth way of talking to the ladies, but in the end, it was me who was making it happen.

When it was all over, these trips would end in all of us blasting the radio as loud as we could get it while head banging to our favorite tunes. Sometimes when I close my eyes at night, I think

of those days and how things used to be. Whatever happened to that friendship and innocence? What ever happened to loving your life and just being a kid? Was anyone listening to the heartaches that we all possessed inside? I felt every night that I went to bed that it could possibly be my last. Nothing was ever panning out, and ever since Cindy B. left and I got kicked out of Milton for the last time, I knew that I had to start living life on the edge. The actions started to tumble on top of everything, and it only got worse from there. The more involvement I had with Kenny and Ricky, the harder a person I became, looking to set the world afire.

All of my frustrations seemed to slip away when we would head out to the Selinsgrove pool. I'd do my laps and let my emotions swim free with me also. Those hot summer days would just have a way of taking my mind away. It was very therapeutic for me to get out and do this. The water caressing my face and body seemed to have all of the answers. Sometimes I would wish I was out at sea, just absorbing all that lay in front of me with no one else out there to look at me like a freak. Total freedom. That's what I truly craved: total freedom.

After taking our laps in the pool, Kenny, Ricky, and I would try to get a few cute girls to come out and play some three-on-three with us in

basketball. This didn't seem to be as hard as we originally thought because these girls were prancing around in there tight cut bikinis and wanted attention desperately. And we were more than happy to give it to them whenever they desired.

Of course, each time we would play any girls, we would let them win because it kept them around just a little bit longer. The best part of the whole ordeal would be getting the opportunity to rub up against the girls while we were playing. I think every single one of us guy's was getting a hard on every time those soft asses would bounce off of our crotch. I don't think the girls minded it either because they would continue to play along and keep up with their cute smiles and inability to shoot a ball in the basket.

Soon afterwards, there was parade in Selinsgrove so all of us headed out there for that. The chatting with the people I knew and the pizza eating was going the way I had hoped, but what was to follow is what made this evening memorable.

While walking around, I bumped into a girl I knew by the name of Nicole. We decided to walk around, and after awhile she asked me to come back to her place. Without any hesitation, I agreed. Once we arrived at her house, we decided to stay out in the kitchen because her parents were in the

living room, and she couldn't have boys alone in her room.

After a few minutes of fooling around, she decided she wanted to start going down on me. My heart was racing. What if her parents walked in? The sweat started swimming down my body, and my mind was going in a million different directions. Her sucking became harder and harder, and without feeling it come, I blew my load right into her mouth. Did she swallow? She sure as fuck did, and this ended up being one of the best days of my life. From that day forward, I have had an appreciation for parades. Thank you, Nicole.

When it seemed things weren't going as planned, they would take a turn and put me on the right track. Harry had a 1986 Camaro for sale, and I was willing, with the help of my parents and the money that I had kept from my ordeal with the professor, to buy it off of him. That mother fucking thing could run beautifully, and it sure as hell would turn any head that we were driving past. We used that car in every position we could, from driving through the streets of Milton, to going up to Williamsport and even through Selinsgrove.

I felt like I was in heaven. People would get me to take them for rides to places they needed to be. I only had my learner's permit at that point, but

I never got busted for it, thank God. This allowed us to hit up the swimming pool in Selinsgrove whenever we wanted. The places we would head to up in Williamsport often times made us quite nervous. We never knew what we would get ourselves into. After a few incidents of running into people staring at us like we fell out of the sky, not to mention their slick comments, we finally stopped heading up there. Feeling like our safety was at risk just wasn't worth it to either of us.

On our last trip home from Williamsport, we stopped at a Perkins restaurant where trouble would surely find us. It all started out as fun as could be. I began by making jokes and everyone was having a really good time. To keep the mood alive, I decided to act like I worked there and went over and picked up the menu and tried waiting on some tables. This went on for a little bit until the waitress soon realized what was truly going on. She came over to our table a little agitated but was calmed down once her boss came over and reassured her. She thought it was very funny. The nice black woman, who was the manager, let me know just how much she enjoyed watching me mess around with the workers that she actually gave me a free meal.

Apparently, my friends weren't as smart as I once thought. After having an amusing kind of day

with Kenny, Ricky, and the girls we met up with in Williamsport, things started to take a turn for the worse. Feeling comfortable in his own ridiculous way, Kenny pointed out a random guy and told him to suck his cock. Groping himself while telling the man to portray such action, the random guy flipped the fuck out.

Sprinting towards us, he grabbed a hold of Kenny and started beating the living shit out of him. The fighting continued to get worse, and I could feel my blood start to get warm and scared. I couldn't handle the situation, so I looked out in the distance like a deer in headlights. What to do, I kept thinking to myself. Before I had a moment to react, one of the girls we were with reached into the glove compartment and pulled out a gun. She pointed it right at the man beating Kenny and threatened to, in her exact words, 'blow his mother fucking brains out.'

Everything drastically turned from that point on. The man removed himself from Kenny and slowly started to back away. My eyes and words were frozen, and I couldn't think of anything to say at all. Everyone was stopped dead in their tracks without a single word spoken. Kenny looked at me with his face in a bloody condition and eventually looked away in disgust.

Then he started screaming at me, 'why the fuck didn't you do something, Norm? Why the fuck didn't you do something?' I didn't know what to say and stayed frozen in my tracks. I thought to myself, what about Ricky. What about him not doing anything? What did he expect me to do that he held exception to Ricky? At this point, it didn't even matter. The girl held herself in complete slow motion trying to figure out what she had just done. She didn't blink for the rest of the night. We all kind of just got back into the car and drove off. Later on she would mention that she considered it my fault that it went too far. She expected me to grab the gun or the fist from the guy that was hitting Kenny. In my opinion, Kenny got exactly what was coming to him. When you act like a complete idiot, then complete consequences are bound to follow, I thought. That night was the last time that I would see those girls, and that was just fine with me.

I thought about a quote from the outsiders that I was very fond of. "You can't win. You know that, don't you? It doesn't matter if you whip us; you'll still be where you were before, at the bottom. And we'll still be the lucky ones at the top with all the breaks. It doesn't matter. Greasers will still be Greasers and Socs will still be Socs. It doesn't matter."

That's how I felt about that whole ordeal. It didn't matter what I would or wouldn't do in this life because I'd always be the loser. It was easy enough for me when I was around my friends to act like I was tough and that others' actions had impact. Sometimes I'd sit and wonder whether or not my acting was as fake as the smile on all of my friends' faces.

Chapter 9
Problem Child

The next couple of weeks went by without much of a sound between Kenny, Ricky, and me. That was until football season came rolling around again, and we all decided to head out to a few games. Our usual football adventures would lead us to the Selinsgrove games. We liked going there because we became familiar around their pool and basketball courts. Also, we didn't have the discomfort of being around anyone from Milton and hearing the usual bullshit that often times plagued every single good time. A lot of the times we four would act tough and sit there and try to talk to all certain kinds of people. And you know what? Most of the time that indeed worked, and it felt nice.

For the first time since our little scare in Williamsport, we all decided it was time we tried our hand at the Lycoming mall again. The next few months of visits there went by as smooth and calm as possible. We'd hurtle in my 86' Camaro and get there as soon as we could. The arcade was our one and only stomping ground there. Piling up as many

tickets as we could to win the prizes shown on the wall, it was a race to see who could possibly get the most. Even though the prizes we were winning weren't anything spectacular, yet it was still a thrill to win.

I wasn't always winning in the games, but no one was taking me down when it came to pool. No one could beat me. It was though I was unstoppable and nothing could possibly slow me down, except for a few slices of pizza and a gallon of Pepsi. Still though, I was a force to be reckoned with. One of the times some guy in his group of friends came over and decided that they were going to run me out of the game by placing a little wager. Nervous at first with my lip quivering just a little, I said, "Maybe."

"What's the matter, puss?" one kid flared back at me.

Bobby looked over to me and said, "You better play him, Norm. You know you are too good to back down."

Taking Bobby's advice, I decided it was time to man up and do this. The first game dragged on a bit before I eventually won.

"Beginners luck,' the kid said.

"How about another game?" I answered back. This continued until the poor kid couldn't

take losing anymore. Five games. Yeah, that's how many games I managed to kick his ass. These trips back and forth to the Lycoming mall went on for weeks. It was some of the funnest times in my life.

I still remember in 1993, when my car was in the shop, I had really wanted to go to the Lycoming mall to continue my reign of terror on the pool table. Unfortunately, finding a ride was becoming harder and harder because of the weather outside. The roads were clouded in heavy snow and weren't driveable, but I managed to talk Harry into taking Ricky, Kenny, and me there anyhow.

After finally arriving there, the mall announces that they will be closing down in half an hour. The expressions on everyone's faces were priceless. The red burning up in their face could have fried me. 'What the fuck, Norman?' It sure wasn't the first time that I had heard that being announced. Now we had to turn around and go back home. I felt like a complete loser and rightfully so, putting all of our lives on the line like that. It was stupid. Thankfully, no one got hurt.

The ride home was a silent one with Harry trying to find the road and Ricky and Kenny trying not to beat the hell out of me. Soon enough though, our friendships would start to turn sour.

Shane Hoffman

Chapter 10
And Justice for All….. Or so they say

You never know when you're going to live one of those days when it changes the rest of your life…the moment that defines you. It's a reaction that decides for itself just exactly who you are. We all have times in our lives when we regret and question every single choice that we make. Somewhere in my path in life I've grown fond of the quote "Love is what we are born with; Fear is what we learned here."

Thursday, December 8th, 1993 - Friday, December 9th

I was hanging out at Harry Young's trailer most of the day when he decided to take me home. When I got home, I went into my room to get some alone time for awhile. Sitting under my bed was a knife I had recently purchased on a trip to New York City with my mom and her coworkers. The knife came out of one of those trade shops in Manhattan. For the next few moments, I sat crossed legged on my bed just gazing into it. The reason for

purchasing it was a mixture of showing it off to my friends and having a little security with me when I got picked on.

Knock. Knock. Knock. Rushing to the door, I looked through the peep hole and saw Bobby standing outside asking if he could come in. 'Of course,' I said as he stepped into my house. 'You want to go riding around with Ricky after his dad gets off to work?' Without much hesitation I agreed. 'Sure, why not,' was my exact answer. And with that, the circus finally begins.

Heading down to the Arm Bar, we both sit on the railroad tracks, waiting for Ricky to pick us up. Bullshitting the time away, I decided to take out the knife and show it to Bobby to see what type of response I could get from him. A smile came across his face, and he said, 'cool.' It was one of those smiles where he genuinely appreciated what he just saw. Hoping no one would see us with it, I quickly hide it under my leg.

Finally, arriving to pick us up, Ricky came speeding onto the street, squealing his tires, his latest attempt at trying to show off in front of us. Big deal, I thought. When we hopped into his car, he didn't exactly know where we were heading, but we managed our way out of Milton and onto some road in New Columbia. Not much talking was

going between the three of us, just the radio and our glancing around at everything that was dead around. All of a sudden, Ricky spun off to the side of the road and pulled out a starter pistol. He then jammed the gun to the side of Bobby's head and pulled the trigger. Startling Bobby, Ricky began to laugh, saying he only did it because he heard that if you did it like that, it would cause a lot of discomfort to the person's ear, mainly the eardrum.

Finally, growing weary of sitting there listening to himself laugh, Ricky finally started driving away. After only a few miles into the other direction, we pull into a Uni-Mart in Watsontown. Bobby and Ricky wanted to go inside to grab some matches for whatever reason. While they were both inside, I snuck the knife into the glove compartment of Ricky's car. Hoping no one saw me, I acted like I was doing something else to cause no attention to me. Successfully completed, I saw them come out of the store. They seemed to be arguing but only in a playful sense at the moment.

We then started driving away, and it only took a few moments for us to see an opportunity for trouble. There was an old woman coming out of the laundromat in Watsontown, and we all had the thought dancing in our minds that we should rob her. Hey, there's no one around, and we could

easily get away with it, we thought. After pulling into the parking lot, we started to devise a plan to do it quick and easy. Fortunately, when the time came, we all chickened out and decided it was best that we didn't hurt the old woman. If that only stopped the chaos to follow, this wouldn't be being read right now.

Cruising back into Milton, Ricky pulled into a Coastal Mart on Broadway. As we were climbing out of the car, Ricky and Bobby got into the same confrontation from before, and Bobby locked all the doors, refusing to come out. So as Ricky and I continued our way into the store, I made my way out. Bobby had just gotten out of the car. Checking Ricky's glove compartment out, I realized that my knife was missing. It was in Bobby's hands. After Bobby and Ricky exchanged a few words, Bobby threatened to use it to stab Ricky. Surprisingly, the lady working behind the desk screamed at him to put it away and get out of the store because she had a bigger one and would use it. Scared at the moment, they both hurried on out of the store. Feeling awkward in the car with the dead silence, Bobby just put the knife down on the floor of the vehicle.

Then it's time for us to head on over to James Hasbin's house. Not wanting to be there

at all but feeling too scared after what had just occurred, I decided to go along with it and go into his house. Everything started out as planned, just a few guys sitting around and bullshitting with one another. Then the talking turned into a sexual one right before my eyes.

James Hasbin came back into the living room with a chair for me to sit on. Refusing at first, all three of them Ricky, Bobby, and James threatened to kick my ass and kill me if I didn't sit in this chair. Old emotions and memories started to surface like a bad prom date, and I could feel my skin start to crawl and my heart start to race.

All three of them now had their cocks hanging out, and they started jerking them. I then started giving them oral sex. Their moans and little smirks had my blood turning inside. Going down the row, one dick at a time, my feelings of worthlessness and shame are now the only feelings I knew. And they stayed. Soon after, James took me into his room where he made me slowly lick his nipples. He said this was the only way he got really hard and horny. After that, I started fucking him in the ass. It felt nasty and common at this point in my life. He yelled for me to continue. He apparently liked it.

Bobby peeked into the door and now wanted to be able to do it to James and then have it done to him, but James wouldn't let him and neither Ricky nor I were going to do it for the fact that Bobby hadn't always been the cleanest person around. In a ray of fury, Bobby stormed out of the house and headed out to the parking lot behind the Rockwell center. Bobby's rage was only getting worse, and I tried to chase after him to calm him down. Once I finally caught up to him, we tried to have a conversation, but that ended quickly when he made it apparent that he wasn't willing to talk at the moment.

We continued our usual shenanigans by looking through peoples' cars in the lot, hoping to find some extra cash. Ricky found a few dollars here and there. Bobby found much of the same, and I managed to get a total of ten dollars until some guy spotted us and started yelling that he was calling the cops. We took off on a dead sprint and actually got away with it, making the moment feel a little more accomplished. To make sure we didn't get caught, we ran back to Ricky's vehicle and headed out to Chef Boyardee's.

Ricky dropped Bobby and me off at the corner by the old firehouse on the corner of Liberty Avenue and the other street, which I can't remember

anymore. Heading our way down the railroad tracks to get home quicker, Bobby decided to stop and talk to me finally. He told me he wanted me to suck his dick, and he continued by getting his penis out, shaking it at me. I felt a quick burst of hurt and anger. What the fuck was he doing this for? He knew how badly I'd been hurt by the preacher in the island and now by our two so-called friends. What was he fucking thinking? I screamed at the top of my lungs 'NO! NO! NO!' He began to laugh and pulled his dick back into his pants and ran ahead of me. Running after him as fast as I could, Bobby picked up a few rocks and began to throw them at me. Some of them hit me and some didn't. In a moment when I began to fear that I would get hurt, I decided to tackle him when he bent down to pick up some more.

Out of the corner of my eye, I see Ricky running behind me. He had decided to come with us now instead of go home. I finally tackled Bobby onto the ground. I reached back to punch him in the face, but he moved just in time, and I missed and hit my hand on the ground. He then bit down right on my thumb, the pain shooting through me like thunder. Thinking the only way I could get him to let go, I pulled out the knife with my other hand and stabbed him two times in the chest.

All of a sudden, I felt Ricky tackle me. As I tried to get back up, Ricky punched me right in the nose, causing it to to bleed profusely.

"What the fuck was that for? I screamed at him.

"Leave Bobby alone!" Ricky sharply shoots right back. Now believing that Ricky was there to help him, Bobby let him try to help him up. Ricky told me to grab a hold of Bobby and help. My anger and fury was still pounding through me at this point, but I did as he said.

When Ricky had tackled me, it caused me to lose control of the knife, allowing Ricky to grab it instead.

My grip on Bobby lead me to hold him to the telephone pole, and Ricky continued the stabbing, causing the blood to pour right out of Bobby. I was keeping myself away from the knife as much as possible, hoping not to get stabbed. I escaped without any stab wounds. I could hear Bobby pleading for his life as his last moments were filled with sheer pain, the knife continuing to go in and out of him. The blood-thirsty anger was almost done.

Feeling almost paralyzed, I let Bobby go and he managed to pull himself off the ground and run a few feet until Ricky caught up to him and

continued the stabbing once again. I looked into the soul of Bobby's eyes and saw pure terror in there. He was lost and alone with no one helping him. I was now lying down on the tracks, shaking, hoping that I was not going to be stabbed next.

The sound of Bobby's last cries rang in my ears: "Please stop. Please stop. God, I don't want to die. I don't want to die."

Ricky stood up and began kicking him in the face, screaming at him with the words, "You won't tell anyone now, will you? You won't tell anyone now, will you? Are you dead yet?"

I finally started screaming, pleading Ricky to stop. At first he didn't, but then it was over. Ricky's anger had stemmed from earlier in the day when Bobby told him he was going to tell everyone about Ricky's gay sex for money and that he did it just for fun. Ricky did a good job of keeping that lifestyle of his hidden and wasn't going to risk letting it all get out.

Ricky then ran home as I walked over to Bobby's body and saw that he wasn't moving. He was dead. My friend was dead. And it was due to the anger and rage of Ricky and me. Wake up, Bobby. Wake up. The earth began to move rapidly under my feet, and I felt the winter air take a hold of my senses. Every body part I had was numb at

the moment. I couldn't feel my feet or fingers, and my eyes were forever indented on Bobby's dead bloody body, lying there exposed for the animals. In another moment of desperation, I sprinted to Ricky's house.

When I arrived at his place, his mother was there to answer the door. Inviting me inside, suddenly Ricky came out with different clothes on, and as I put my hand on his shoulder, he told me to go downstairs for some sleep and he would see me in the morning.

Lying on his downstairs sofa, my mind was running a million miles per hour with teardrops the size of golf balls sprinting down my face. Bobby's dead, I thought. Bobby's dead. I wondered what was to come next. Nothing of significance ran through my mind. The only thing I kept thinking about was that if I stayed at home like my mother told me to, this would have never happened. He would still be alive, and I wouldn't be without him and that entire dick sucking throughout the day wouldn't have happened. I wouldn't have had to give anal sex and watch again as my life slipped away.

The next morning finally came, and Ricky met me downstairs with some different clothing to wear. I went out to breakfast with my mother.

Little did I know, Ricky was making plans for his alibi and pin me down for the murder. Calling Kenny, he explained how I killed Bobby and that he did what he could do to stop me. Kenny was always closer to Ricky than me so he immediately took what he said as facts and nothing else. He stood by his side too.

My mother dropped me off at Ricky's when we were done, and I met him and Kenny there. Ricky continued right in front of me to explain to Kenny exactly what I did to kill Bobby. Their eyes were cynical and I was afraid to disagree with them. What if he decided to kill me next? What if Kenny was in on it too? My fear took a hold of my heart, and I managed once again in life to keep my mouth shut.

We next climbed into Ricky's car and made our way to Harry's trailer, and on the way Ricky pointed out to Kenny where Bobby's body was lying. They asked me to stay at Harry's trailer so they could go see if Heather Young was home, but she wasn't so then they decided to drive back and pick me up. All of us headed out to the mall to get something to eat and play some games. This time was obviously different from the rest. Not only was Bobby no longer with us, but I was rarely spoken too. Ricky and Kenny were acting like nothing had

happened and were continuing on like it was no big deal that Ricky and I had killed Bobby the night before.

I decided to call one of our friends, Lester Hunt, for my birthday presents, so we left and stopped at Lester's house, and I got my present. It was a bag full of pennies. Afterwards, we drove to the trailer court in Milton, and Kenny threw away a bag of clothes, which I figured were the clothes that Ricky and I were wearing the night before during the killing. Right after this, they both dropped me off at my house and drove away.

After arriving home, it wasn't too long after when the cops arrived at my house and asked my mom to take me down to the police station. It wasn't too long after my mother and I got there that the cops placed me under arrest for the murder of Robert Coup. Right before I was placed under arrest for murder, two of the investigating cops that questioned me only asked me three questions: do you smoke, drink, or do drugs? Nothing about the murder was asked of me, and my answer to all of the questions was the obvious no. My heart was going through the ceiling, and I didn't know what to do so I remained silent. My silence was the only thing I ever did when I got scared. I always figured if I didn't say anything, I couldn't get into trouble or be

hurt, but I was starting to realize my silence had run and destroyed my entire life up to this point.

The two investigating officers should have never been allowed to question me or arrest me because they were related to both of the main witnesses. Officer Bud Dugan's and Ken Royer's relations to Ricky and Kenny should have taken them right off the case. If that's not a conflict of interest, then I truly don't know what is. The cops thrived off the details of Ricky and Kenny. Milton was a small town full of people willing to do anything to get attention. The cops didn't know anything about the case and weren't interested in listening to what I had to say. For them, getting a quick arrest was much more important. Whether or not it was the right one, didn't matter at all. It made them look like geniuses, getting an arrest that quickly, putting them right in the spotlight of the headlines for days to come. Congratulations Milton Police and community; you managed to fuck it up once again.

Kenny only knew what Ricky told him because he was never there. He knew that my background would be easier for the cops to pin me down for the murder, and his relationship with Ricky went much deeper than ours. Therefore, Kenny should have never been a main witness.

Also if I did indeed commit the murder, then Ricky and Kenny would have had plenty of time to get a hold of the cops when I left Ricky's place in the morning.

Instead the cops only started getting answers when a truck driver discovered the body and informed the authorities. Their stories didn't line up with each other, and like I mentioned, if they knew I did it and truly believed it, then why didn't they take the perfect opportunity to nail me on it. It should have never come down to a truck driver finding the body. Once that happened and the cops got involved, Ricky panicked and with the alibi of Kenny, sealed his innocence. Kenny was willing to go along with it to protect his friend.

I can still recite the lines out of the Standard Journal about the killing when they mentioned me. It was priceless and truly didn't add up.

"Authorities believe Coup died at about 1 a.m. Thursday, following a scuffle. They don't know the motive or why Gundrum allegedly "lost it." They found a great deal of deadly apparent knife wounds, Sacavage said, and police received good information from the teenagers who were with Gundrum. Sacavage said there have been some rumors that Gundrum has been involved in

some minor incidents, but there was nothing in the past that would have pegged him as a walking time bomb."

Shane Hoffman

Chapter 11
18 and Life
(CQ-6130)

"My client pleads guilty," was my attorney's opening statement in the trial. I guess what was irritating about that was that I never said I *was* guilty. More so, I never told him to say that. Huddled around the table before the trial started, my lawyer, whom my grandmother put all of her savings into saving my life, opened up with 'my client pleads guilty.' His reasoning was that the jury and judge might not come at me as hard if I confessed and tried to explain my reasoning for what I had done.

The problem with that is I didn't take the stand in my own trial. I couldn't. I can't do this, I told myself. My mind and emotions were paralyzed with fear and despair. In all of my life, I've been too scared to speak out, and then at the most crucial time, I faltered. Not giving myself the opportunity to help myself proved to be the greatest mistake of all. My attorney's next big move was to tell the court that I killed Bobby Coup, but it wasn't on purpose. The goal was to convince the court that

even though I killed him, I had lost total control at the time and didn't know what I was doing. The problem with that that is that I didn't kill him with that intention. My stabbing came at him twice, and they were to get him to stop gnawing on my thumb. The moment I lost control is when Ricky intervened and punched me. I, with my mind being as distorted as it was, grabbed Bobby and put him on that telephone pole to be stabbed to death. It was out of fear that I was going to be killed if I didn't follow through with the orders.

When it was time for Ricky to take the stand, he did a wonderful job at making everyone eat out of his hands. His telling of how I killed Bobby raced through everyone. There wasn't a doubt amongst anyone that I did kill Bobby. My fate was sealed from that point on. It wasn't over yet though. Kenny had his chance to take the stand and make himself out to be the one that was concerned about me. The court didn't understand that Kenny only knew what Ricky told him. Never at any point during the murder was Kenny present whatsoever. It also helped a great deal that one of the officers for Milton was Ricky's relative. None of this was brought out into the court, and it should have. If so, I might not have ended up in this predicament I'm in.

Ricky had the chance to speak to the police and take a deal. It involved me being thrown under the bus and him walking away. He provided the details and got charged with only lying. Yeah, you're fucking right he was lying...lying about me and that entire night. Still though, I sat there cold in my seat, afraid to move the slightest inch.

What kept me so damn scared? What was it that made me feel like I was going to make the situation worse? Couldn't I see that I was getting ready to have my life be over with? I felt so ashamed and lost inside myself that I didn't know how to cope with it. Creating that childhood fantasy in my mind got me through most of it. The stares of the people were so cold that I could almost feel my body temperature dropping at an alarming rate. I just wanted to close my eyes and have it all go away, but it wouldn't. It would only get progressively worse by each passing second.

Another knife right into my heart was seeing how upset all of this made my then girlfriend, Kristy. Kristy was the beautiful girl that was ready to fuck me whenever and however I wanted. The girl had a libido that would give Charlie Sheen a run for his money. She also loved me and treated me like I had never been treated before. Her caring loving touch would make me feel like living when

the worst of my life would reoccur. It was starting to become evident to her that we would never see each other again. Kristy even stayed by my side when she found out that I cheated on her once with another girl. Till this day, I can't think of one logical reason why I would hurt someone that loves me. I guess the saying "hurt people hurt people" is true. When you have been hurt and kicked around your entire life, the only thing you know how to do is hurt another person whether it is intentional or not. It's just the way that we live.

The look on her mother's face was hard also. When she took the stand to hear that her daughter was having sex with me, it disgusted her. To know her daughter was having sex with a brutal cold hearted killer was too much for her to bear. That's what the system wants you to think. They want you to forget that when someone is on trial, his is a walking, breathing human being with emotions and love. They want you to look down upon the person and cast judgments. They want you to belittle that person and look at him like he is some worthless piece of trash. Every criminal in this world they do that to, whether it's a large or small criminal. That's just the world we live in. This all too was true for her mother, and I don't blame her for one second

because the way I was being made out to be in court would put that expression on my face too.

During the trial, they wanted to make me out to be a kid who was a ticking time bomb that was about to explode. And when I exploded, I decided to take my frustrations out by brutally murdering Bobby Coup because he was starting to have a good life. Those in the courts should each have their own little television program like Judge Judy because they sure are entertaining. They can take any man and make him out to be whatever they please. And with me that was exactly what they did, except I was made out to be a fucking monster.

Not too many people took the stand to speak positively on my behalf. And it finally showed when the verdict came in. As it was getting ready to be announced, my palms got sweaty, and I started to shake with teardrops getting ready to race down my face.

"Norman Gundrum, Jr., we find you guilty for the murder of Robert Coup."

My heart felt like it was falling out of my chest, and my eyes are too blurry to see. The earth around me had stopped spinning, and from that moment forward, I was inmate CQ-6130. And that's how it would stay for the rest of my life.

When the sentencing finally got around, two years had passed by. My debt to society and Robert's family was 18 and life with no parole. Nothing. No chance at parole to speak my side of the story. No chance of ever seeing the light of day. No chance at ever getting laid by a pretty girl again. My life is a small cell located in Coal Township, PA.

My mother visits me every once in awhile and my grandparents, the Dershem's, visit me every month. A beautiful girl named Alicia used to visit me too until she had to get on with her life out in the real world. It gets really lonely in here, and I often times dream of getting out and doing the right thing. Every single day that goes by I think about how I helped end Bobby's life and how I destroyed a large part of the lives of his family. You ask me what I was thinking and how I could have done such a stupid thing. I don't know. I just don't know how. It happened quickly, and when it happened, my mind wasn't processing him being dead and never having the chance to grow up and have kids and enjoy his life.

A young man's life was taken for no reason. A human life was robbed out of a moment of desperation. I loved Bobby. I truly did. He was my best friend, and he knew it. We think as we are

children that we are allowed to do whatever we please, and there is going to be no consequences for our actions. I was only fifteen years old when I helped kill Bobby. Not for one second did I stop and think about my own life and desires. My goals and dreams were to not be who I was but instead be someone who others loved and desired. If any of those thoughts would have crossed my mind, Bobby would still be alive. Remember that sometimes in the spur of the moment, you may do something that will change your life forever. And once it happens. you can't take it back. It's final. I'd do anything to change positions with Bobby and give him the opportunity that was wrongfully taken.

My first three days I was in lockdown with a guard and his sandwich. It was cold and dark, and it smelled of a nasty fungus. I can't handle this, I thought to myself. My fear was now at a different kind of high, and it was one where I truly only had myself to handle it. I spent most of that time sleeping and trying to convince myself that it wasn't real, just a dream. Yeah, that is what it was...just a dream. If that were only the case for me. Sometimes when your life hits rock bottom, you need to laugh to keep from crying. Reality didn't start sitting in that I would do life in prison until a few years later. It has become immune to me anymore. It's just a

way of life, a way of life that I wouldn't wish upon anyone else, but for me, it's what I know. And to tell you the truth, most days in here are a lot better than days I had on the outside.

I started to spend all of my time playing basketball and cards. It became my escape on the inside, the way to drift away and not be bothered. Another world in another dimension, I liked to think of it. People ask if there is anything that I regret on a daily basis. Yeah, I sure definitely regret a lot in life. What I regret everyday is the pain and loss I caused Bobby Coup and his family. I really have two outlooks on life. I hope to get out someday and live a normal life and become a productive member of society. I would also like to get involved with helping to keep juveniles out of trouble and just be there for my family.

Some people win in this world, and some people lose. The winners are those that in the face of disaster pick themselves off the ground and keep going. Those who lose never get back up. They live in the face of what they lived through and drown in it. They never let themselves see the light of day because their minds are too fixated in the past.

Often times I wonder whatever happened to some of the people I went to school with and the girls I dated. My mind focuses on heaven a lot and

I'm a born again Christian. I believe Jesus Christ loves me and does indeed have a plan for me. I have to believe that. It's not only a way of surviving but a way of living. I'll leave you with a quote from the movie a Bronx tale.

"I learned to give love and get love unconditionally. You just have to accept people for what they are, and I learned the greatest gift of all. The saddest thing in life is wasted talent, and the choices that you make will shape your life forever. But you can ask anybody from my neighborhood, and they'll just tell you this is just another Bronx tale." Timeline

Norman Gundrum, Jr., who is serving a life sentence for murder, accused Bucknell professor Jack Harclerode along with Lester Hunt and Harry Young in 1995 of sexually abusing him. The two men were charged and plea bargained out, however, the DA of the county at the time said there was not enough evidence to bring charges against the professor. The professor retired a couple years later and paid a $25K settlement to Norman two years after that.

On Jan. 25, 1995, just two days after Mr. Gundrum testified at his sentencing, state

trooper David Darrough, now a corporal, began an investigation into Mr. Gundrum's allegations against Mr. Harclerode, Mr. Hunt and Mr. Young.

Mr. Hunt and Mr. Young were eventually charged with felony involuntary deviate sexual intercourse as a result of Mr. Gundrum's claims that he was abused by both men in 1992 when he was 15.

The felony charges were dropped in exchange for guilty pleas to corruption of a minor, and both Mr. Hunt and Mr. Young were jailed for a few months in Northumberland County Prison.
On June 30, 1997, Mr. Harclerode retired from Bucknell University after 32 years.

In February of 1999, Mr. Harclerode offered Mr. Gundrum a one-time $20,000 payment or $25,000, with interest, over four years to settle the suit against him and his former employer, according to documents obtained by The Daily Item.

Mr. Gundrum accepted the $25,000 and agreed to release Mr. Harclerode and the university from any further action, suits, or demands, according to the settlement release dated April 7, 1999.

The document, signed by Mr. Harclerode and Mr. Gundrum, states the retired professor agreed to pay the convicted murderer four payments totaling

$27,250 to settle the suit against him and Bucknell University.

The fourth, and final, settlement check of $6,625 was sent April 10, 2002, to Mrs. Dersham, trustee of the Norman R. Gundrum, Jr. Trust.

A copy of the check from the Lewisburg law firm, Brann & Light, which represented Mr. Harclerode in the civil case, specifies the money is for "Harclerode's final settlement payment."

In March 2007, the professor was arrested on molestation charges stemming from an incident with a 10-year-old boy.

In May 2007, police filed additional charges for child pornography that was found on the professor's computer.

In January of 2008, the professor entered a guilty plea to indecent sexual assault for the molestation charges; he was sentenced in February of this year to 9-30 months in prison followed by 36 months of probation. He was also to register as sexually violent predator.

In April of 2008, the professor was charged based on allegations by a man who claimed he was repeatedly sexually assaulted from 1992-1995, beginning when the man was 12 years old. This case is still pending.

In December of 2008, the professor pleaded guilty to 20 counts of possession of child pornography. He was sentenced to 13 years to 27 1/2 years in prison.

His daughter testified in the sentencing trial in January that he admitted to her that he had had sexual contact with prepubescent boys in the 1960's, 1970's, 1980's, and 1990's, including a 12-year-old named Norman Gundrum.

Since receiving the financial settlement, Mr. Gundrum has contributed to numerous charities and organizations, including the annual Needy Family Fund co-sponsored by The Daily Item/Danville News; Milton Area School District's booster club; the former Kauffman Public Library in Sunbury and the Pennsylvania Crime Victims Compensation Fund.

Despite the investigation and financial settlement, Mr. Harclerode was given emeritus status from Bucknell University when he retired 10 years ago.

As of today, Mr. Norman Gundrum, Jr. is serving a life sentence in prison.

Accomplishments

Since Mr. Gundrum's life sentence, he has accomplished the following:

G.E.D/ High School Diploma

Associate's degree in Paralegal Studies, The Paralegal institute of Arizona

Started Scholarship in Robert Coup's memory at Milton High School

Donated to Make-A-Wish foundation

Donated to the Office of Victim's Services in Harrisburg

Certificate D.M.M. Operation Principles

Certificate Cooper Busman Construction Safety

Certificate of Carpentry level one and two

Certificate Electronics Systems Technician level one and two

Certificate Electrical level one

Certificate Core Curriculum N.C.C.E.R.

Certificate of Construction Site Safety Orientation

Graduate Crossroads Bible Institute Bible Study Program in (Grandville, MI)

Won numerous holiday tournaments: Gin, Volleyball, and Basketball

Certificate of participation from 2004-2009 in shoot to swish for the Make- A- Wish foundation

Certificate bible study course from Gospel Express Evangelistic team

Currently most money raised at one time at SCI-Coal Township

Certificate Proliteracy America tutor training

Certificate Laubach Literacy action tutor training

Certificate life care program (Bethesda Family Services Found)

Diploma legal assistant/paralegal diploma program Blackstone career institute final grade of 96/12%

Wrote numerous letters to troubled juveniles

Won numerous championships in sports: softball, volleyball, and basketball

On the volleyball all-star team that plays a team from the outside for the past eight years

Diploma certified legal assistant program (paralegal institute in Arizona)

Achievement awards from the paralegal institute in Arizona in the following: Fundamentals of Psychology 101, Legal Research, English 102 technical writing.

Certificate stress and anger management class

Certificate youthful offender's program

Certificate health and wellness class

Certificate PA Dept. of Education Pre Voc Class

Active member in SCI-Coal Townships Inmate Organization (Triumph)

3 credits from Saint Francis of Pa College

Pa D.O.C Run-A-Thon participated in one way or another for seven years.

Certificates for his participation in the Run-A-Thon

Certificate in Beginner Video Production Class

Certificate Health Education Program at SCI-Camp Hill

Certificate Beginner Yoga and Stretching Class

Certificate free as an Eagle Religious Class

Certificate for Baptism here at SCI-Coal Township

Certificate Citizenship Course SCI-Coal Township

Certificate money smart class SCI-Coal Township

Certificate legal reference aide training SCI-Coal Township

Took impact of crime class

Written articles to the editor

Certificate for thinking for a change class

Graduated building trades class SCI-Coal Township

Graduated Electronics Class SCI-Coal Township

Certificate Beginner Art Class

Construction Safety and Health card from Ossha

Worked as a program Services Janitor

Norman Gundrum has worked as a teacher's aide, law library clerk, commissary worker, mowed grass, shoveled snow, block worker, kitchen worker.

Shane Hoffman

Numerous donations to different people and organizations

Currently working to earn an Associate's degree in Accounting from Ashworth college in Georgia. He has five classes remaining until he graduates.

Acknowledgements

This book is dedicated in the memory of Robert Coup. May you Rest in Peace.

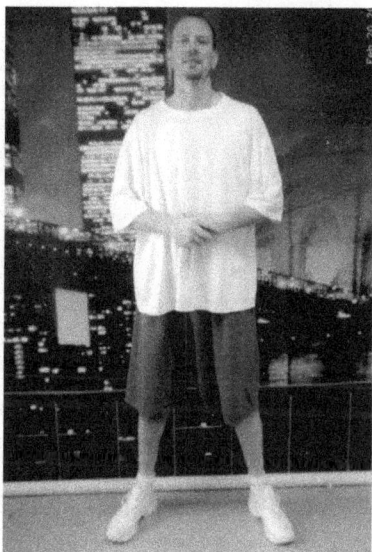

Norman Gundrum, Jr.

www.ingramcontent.com/pod-product-compliance
Lightning Source LLC
Chambersburg PA
CBHW051823040426
42447CB00006B/347